NEW AND SELECTED POEMS

■ ■ ■

1956–1996

ALSO BY PHILIP APPLEMAN

POETRY

New and Selected Poems (University of Arkansas Press, 1996)

Let There Be Light (HarperCollins Publishers, 1991)

Darwin's Bestiary (Echo Press, 1986)

Darwin's Ark (Indiana University Press, 1984)

Open Doorways (W. W. Norton & Company, 1976)

Summer Love and Surf (Vanderbilt University Press, 1968)

Kites on a Windy Day (Byron Press, Nottingham, England, 1967)

FICTION

Apes and Angels (G. P. Putnam's Sons, 1989)

Shame the Devil (Crown Publishers, 1981)

In the Twelfth Year of the War (G. P. Putnam's Sons, 1979)

NONFICTION

The Silent Explosion (Beacon Press, 1965)

EDITED WORKS

Darwin (W. W. Norton & Company, 1970; 1979)

Malthus on Population (W. W. Norton & Company, 1976)

The Origin of Species (W. W. Norton & Company, 1975)

1859: Entering an Age of Crisis (Indiana University Press, 1959)

Victorian Studies (founding co-editor, 1957–63)

NEW AND SELECTED POEMS
■ ■ ■
1956–1996

■ ■ ■
PHILIP APPLEMAN

THE UNIVERSITY OF ARKANSAS PRESS

Fayetteville 1996

00   99   98   97   96   5   4   3   2   1

Designed by Alice Gail Carter

⊛ The paper used in this publication meets the minimum
requirements of the American National Standard for Perma-
nence of Paper for Printed Library Materials   Z39.48-1984.

Library of Congress Cataloging-in-Publication Data

Appleman, Philip, 1926–
      [Poems. Selections]
      New and selected poems, 1956–1996 / Philip Appleman.
          p.   cm.
      Includes bibliographical references and index.
      ISBN 1-55728-419-9 (cloth : alk. paper). —
      ISBN 1-55728-420-2 (pbk. : alk. paper)
      I. Title.
PS3551.P6A6   1996
811'.54—dc20   95-50626
                                        CIP

for Margie

the poetry of my life

who shared the work and the play
and helped make each book

ACKNOWLEDGMENTS

Grateful acknowledgment is made to the following publishers for permission to reprint previously published material:

HarperCollins Publishers: poems from *Let There Be Light*
Indiana University Press: poems from *Darwin's Ark*
W. W. Norton & Company: poems from *Open Doorways*
Vanderbilt University Press: poems from *Summer Love and Surf*
Byron Press: poems from *Kites on a Windy Day*

The title poem of *Darwin's Ark* was rewritten and retitled and is included, under the title "Noah," in the later book, *Let There Be Light*. Slight changes have been made in a few other poems.

Acknowledgment is also made to the editors of the following magazines, where many of these poems first appeared.

American Review, Amicus Journal, Antioch Review, Approach, Arizona Quarterly, Back Door, Beloit Poetry Journal, Bluefish, Chicago Tribune Sunday Magazine, College English, Confrontation, Creel, Denver Post, Dryad, The Fair, Falmouth Review of Literature, Freethought Today, Graffiti, Harper's Magazine, Hawaii Review, The Humanist, Indiana Review, Intervention, Kentucky Poetry Review, The Literary Review, Long Island Quarterly, Malahat Review, Massachusetts Review, Midwest Quarterly, The Nation, New England Review, The New Republic, New York Quarterly, New York Herald Tribune, New York Times, North American Review, North Atlantic Review, The Paris Review, Partisan Review, Pivot, Poetry, Poetry Northwest, Prairie Schooner, Pulp, Quartet, The Reporter, Sewanee Review, Southern California Anthology, Southern Humanities Review, Southern Poetry Review, Spectator, Tendril, Tri-Quarterly, West Coast Review, Wind, Yale Review.

The author wishes to thank the National Endowment for the Arts and the Indiana University Foundation for their support; thanks also to Diana Chang, William Matthews, Miller Williams, Paul Zimmer, and always to my wife, Marjorie H. Appleman, for her inspiration, encouragement, and meticulous editing.

CONTENTS

▪ ▪ ▪ from *Kites on a Windy Day* (1967)

I. THE OUTSIDE

To the River *(Benares)* 3
On the Via Veneto *(Rome)* 5
Snow on the Bosporus *(Istanbul)* 6
Dolphins *(Manzanillo)* 7

II. PROMISES

Crystal Anniversary 8
Vigil 9
A Promise 11

III. TORN KITES

The Knight's Tale 12
Kites on a Windy Day 13
Remembering the Great Depression 14

▪ ▪ ▪ from *Summer Love and Surf* (1968)

I. OLD GLORY

Things to Do with Railroads 16
Success Story 18
Day of the Hawk 19
To the Garbage Collectors in Bloomington, Indiana,
the First Pickup of the New Year 20

II. YOUR LIGHT

Four Measures: Earth, Air, Water, Fire 22
A Poem for St. Valentine's Day 24
Middle of the Night 25
Summer Love and Surf 27

III. SOMEWHERE EAST

At the Nativity Bar and Poolroom *(Bethlehem)*   29
The Path of Renunciation *(Calcutta)*   30
Thinking of Noubli Laroussi *(Algeria)*   31
Three Haiku, Two Tanka *(Kyoto)*   33

IV. LAST CHORDS

A Word to Socrates   35
A Thought for Suse Pollok   36
Last Lines for a Baritone   37
Sweet Life   38
You Said, That's the Fourth Bird This Year to Hit
    Our Picture Window   39

V. THE MEASURE OF ALL THINGS

Butterwort   40
Old Thing   42
Town and Gown   43
Enemy   44

. . . from   *Open Doorways*   (1976)

I. WHERE LIGHT WELLS UP

Memo to the 21st Century   46
Nobody Dies in the Spring   48
Land of Cold Sun   50
Ten Definitions of Lifetime   51
Landing Pattern   53
Kicking Sea Urchins   54
What the U.S. Bureau of Customs Will
    Cry at Public Auction on June 5   56
October Spring   59
The Pill and the Hundred-Yard Dash   60
Bicentennial: The Course of Empire   61
Fighting the Bureaucracy   62

New Year's Resolution   *63*
Seeing into Bedrooms   *65*
"Your Papers, Please"   *67*
East Hampton: The Structure of Sound   *69*

II. BACKS TO THE WALL

Truth   *70*
Westhampton Cemetery   *71*
Serpent   *73*
Revision   *74*
The Tennis Player Waits
     for What Waits for the Tennis Player   *75*
Red Kite   *76*
Central Park: The Anatomy Lesson   *77*
Caravan   *78*
Revolution   *79*
Message ·   *80*
Murder   *82*
For Lucia and the Black Widows of Sperlonga   *83*
Afterward   *89*
Alive   *90*
At the End of the World   *92*

III. SOMETHING IS GONE

On a Morning Full of Sun   *93*
The Persistence of Memory   *94*
Peace with Honor   *95*
Waiting for the Fire   *98*

IV. THE TELLING OF THE HEART

Love Poem   *99*
Ars Poetica   *100*
The Girl Who Hated Threes   *102*
Savior   *104*
Heart of Stone   *105*

Birthday Card to My Mother   *107*
Congenial Poet Desires Intense Relationship
    with Warm, Intelligent Poem   *109*
This Moment   *111*
First Snow   *112*
If Martha Is a Model Mother-in-Law,
    She Is Definitely the Latest Model   *113*
Economics   *115*
In Two Degrees of Cold   *116*
A Kind of Fruitfulness   *118*
Better Half   *119*
Love in the Rain   *120*
Scrapbook   *121*

. . . from   *Darwin's Ark*   (1984)

Preface   *123*

I. GIANTS IN THE EARTH

The Skeletons of Dreams   *126*
Nostalgie de la Boue   *128*
State of Nature   *132*

II. THE RUST OF CIVILIZATIONS

The Hand-Ax   *138*
In Andalucía   *142*
"Black-Footed Ferret Endangered"   *144*
The Faith-Healer Speaks   *145*

III. ANIMALS TAME AND ANIMALS FERAL

Darwin's Bestiary   *150*
    Prologue   *150*
    The Ant   *151*
    The Worm   *152*
    The Rabbit   *153*

The Gossamer   *154*
Euphorias   *155*
    Waldorf-Astoria Euphoria   *155*
    Hunkydoria Euphoria   *157*
How Evolution Came to Indiana   *158*
Mr. Extinction, Meet Ms. Survival   *159*

IV. IN THE CAVES OF CHILDHOOD
    How My Light Is Spent   *161*
    "Sea Otter Survival Assured"   *162*
    On the *Beagle*   *164*
    The Voyage Home   *166*

. . . from   *Let There Be Light*   (1991)

I. THE BIBLE RETOLD FOR GROWNUPS
    Gathering at the River   *173*
    Eve   *175*
    An Eye for an Eye   *177*
    Noah   *178*
    Heavenly Body   *187*
    Sarah   *189*
    Sensual Music   *196*
    Our Tree   *197*
    Gertrude   *198*
    Anniversary   *200*
    The Trickle-Down Theory of Happiness   *201*
    Last-Minute Message for a Time Capsule   *202*

II. INTO THE WIND
    Bildad   *203*
    Night Thoughts   *208*
    David   *209*
    Watching Her Sleep   *211*
    Gifts   *212*

Jonah   *214*

Fleas   *217*

Before You Push the Red Button   *218*

III. THE TREE OF KNOWLEDGE

And Then the Perfect Truth of Hatred   *219*

Mary   *221*

Credo   *224*

Coast to Coast   *226*

Judas   *227*

Heading North   *229*

Martha   *230*

Lighting Your Birthday Cake   *232*

Jesus   *233*

But the Daisies Will Not Be Deceived
    by the Gods   *235*

· · · New Poems

Kissing the Aborigines   *236*

Them   *237*

Eulogy   *238*

Days One through Six, Etc.   *239*

Superstition   *242*

Possessed   *243*

How to Live   *244*

Gravity   *248*

Never-Never Land   *250*

A Priest Forever   *251*

Vasectomy   *256*

Creation   *257*

Will   *258*

Holding On   *260*

· · · Index of Titles   *263*

NEW AND SELECTED POEMS

■ ■ ■

1956–1996

Kites on a Windy Day

TO THE RIVER
(Benares)

For one burning moment
we were snarled together
under the winding-sheet: you,
the boy with blistering eyes,
the brown water-carrier,
the milky lady who walked like a *rani* and sniffed,
and all of us.
The sun was boring through the sheet,
through our eyelids. Strapped cold to the litter,
we hunched on hired shoulders downhill
toward the river, where,
in the whitest white we ever wore,
skinny legs fretting the husky logs,
we would flame to a fine gray ash.
To the equanimity of peacocks
our passing made no tremor;
under the nim and tamarind
burnt eyes died in dusty faces,
monkeys cried abstract abuse,
temples turned their walls on us,
camels wet the earth,
and only children stared, that games and sun
could come to this.
All of us
suddenly
shrieked through the sheet:
My voice is the language of God!
My skin is the color of heaven!
My knowledge makes towers and temples!
My pity, My passion, My deeds!
No one heard.
And

even now, as the litter twists along,
one of us is still there,
swaying to the smug chanting of the mourners,
moving toward fire on the holy river,
one of us.

ON THE VIA VENETO
(Rome)

Rolling hips and rippling breasts
summon the hooves and tails of things.
From hothouse forests of silk and fur,
from thickets of mauve and orange hair,
girls inflame the afternoon,
posturing and leering, till—

Hairy men burst from cypress and pine,
storming the ancient walls, and down
to the billowing bars and boulevards!
Up from the fountains, the rush and swish of scaly men,
the sudden blare of sea-horns wreathed!
And in the streets
a tangle of limbs and torsos! Aiee!
Howls and horns!
Screams!

Delight!

Sun had seen it all before,
bored, departed.
Then hairy men shuddered, scaly men shivered,
rattled and slithered to fountain and pine.

Before the hips began again
to undulate on boulevards,
before another masquerade
of silks and furs and orange hair,
a moment lingered
full of the clatter of cloven hooves,
full of the slip and scour of scales,
and pipes, and wan, triumphant shells
winding in the dusk.

SNOW ON THE BOSPORUS
(Santa Sophia, Istanbul)

I stand across the future, looking back
on all the crooked past. Half blind with snow
I cannot see the shores of Asia, but
phantom ships call strangely through the whirl,
ferries float their hordes from somewhere east
and Hittites and Assyrians swarm ashore
to freeze dominion over all the earth—
and melt along the angry turns of time;
Darius comes, and Xerxes, chain the sea
and lash its insolence—and drown among
gray eddies of the past;
Alexander blunders into
convoluted space; devout
and murderous Crusaders, conquerors
in the name of Allah—all are swept away
in the rush of dim and icy stars.

I stand across the future, looking back
on all my crooked ways, half blind with love
of rectitude and order, chart and graph.
From continent to continent I had hoped
for one triumphant crossing in a line;
but living leaves a wake, and as I stare
at all that vagrant foam, I think again
of Constantine and Kemal, gods and men:
plotting our maps for other futures, we
already know their true-north is askew.
The children of our children will look up
and measure their own stars; for ours will serve
our own time only, dimmer every night
in the gray and swirling blur around our heads,
while Holy Wisdom crieth in the streets.

DOLPHINS

(Manzanillo)

A controversy roiling by the ocean
Imperils friendships with its cold commotion:
When dolphins frisk, is it some sudden swish
Of joy—or are they only after fish?

Most of us are practical; this trammels
Belief in bliss among the other mammals.
But certain dreamy fellows will insist
Gulls hanging in the wind are being kissed,
That breezes nibble at the ears of waves
And whisper rhymes to crabs in craggy caves.

I've seen the rack and scud that spoils a buss
And makes the swish of joy sound ominous;
I know a nibble may become a crunch
And rhymes are poor alternatives to lunch.

But in the noon of sunburned summertime,
When swish and kiss and nibble turn to rhyme,
The dolphins vault into our atmosphere;
And, noting that there are no fishes here,
I lean to those who favor joy, and wish
Delight would dance in my too solid flesh.

CRYSTAL ANNIVERSARY

Deep in a glassy ball, the future looks
Impacted, overdue, a thing that ticks
And dings with promise, but will not happen; we,
Meanwhile, tick-and-dinging through the glow
Of one more married morning, mind the clock
Of age, fading slowly into black-
On-white biographies. The crimson bird
You welcomed sunrise with, and somehow scared,
Has skirred off, blazing, to a hazy past. Still,
It's all there, deep in the glassy ball,
The past as future: you and that morning flash
Of wings bore anniversaries, a rush
Of visions—you, golden on a far-off beach
Sand-silver—anniversary of such
An earlier you, ringed with the flickering churn
Of antique fountains—anniversary again
Of you, you, dazzling in the fever of love
And smiling on those nights we'd hardly move,
But stand for hours, deep in crystal flakes
Of bundled, quiet winter, touching cheeks.
It wasn't then our worst, or yet our best:
It was the first.

VIGIL

Six o'clock. The noise routine has not
Yet started. Shadowy nurses tiptoe in
The muffled hall, a breeze betrays a plot
Against all window shades; but here within
The room things hang limp: the sheet,
A dangling lamp, your filmy feminine
Grotesques—nylon over steel. The heat
Of yesterday has not drained off. I sweat
And wait. The clouds are starting to secrete
A bleary light, meant of course to let
Us know it is the East that sends the sure
Promises of dawn: cigarette
Men, coffee vendors in a truck obscure
And throbbing just outside the window, and
Then nurses with dim smiles. Secure
In sleep behind the black command
NOTHING BY MOUTH, you manage to elude
Them still, doctors, interns, and the planned
Chaos of thermometers, food,
Juices, histories. You sleep. And sleep.

It hasn't started yet. The change of mood
Will come soon enough. But now I keep
My vigil: pondering your peace, I glide
Off quickly to the Peace of God, leap
From there to counting emperors who died
At barbers' hands and in God's peace, proceed
To judgment on the casual homicide
Of metaphysics, and end blessing the deed,
The sanctified fact, the microscope,
And wholly ordered men who intercede
For flesh and bone, in charity and hope;

Faithful to this mood, I feel the Laws
Of Chance come coiling 'round us like a rope.

The spell is hanging in the air like gauze—
The last thing in the world to daunt a nurse.
Her deference is the briefest sort of pause,
And then she shakes you gently, with a terse
"You have a visitor." A heavy night
Of sleep refuses flatly to disperse,
Rolls one way then another till you fight
It off with stretch and twist and solemn yawn.
You see me dark, and you're abruptly bright.
What light is that the morning seizes on?
Not the East. Your waking is the dawn.

A PROMISE

Sunlight tilting into eyes pale china
blue, and hovering, a promise: in this
blue light we swam an August bay,
the glide of water silking past
bare skin; in this December light
we tracked the drops of shadow in the snow
where rabbits ran; this long October sun
angled on our path past shattered homes
of birds in bushes, hands away from earth.

Be careful in this light: in such a slant
you may see trashmen on a tailgate eating
withered apples; you may empty pockets
of the dead and find postage stamps, bus
tokens, blank checks, notebooks—promises;
and in this light, newspapers rustle through
back yards and alleys, tumbling relentlessly
toward something gray and final.

This shelving light has morninged here before,
but never quite like this—now it
promises No, you will never die, you will never,
never die—*this* light, this pale blue
china light, a love sleepy married
light in your pale blue china
Love sleepy china blue eyes.

THE KNIGHT'S TALE

Afterward, in the glow of home fires burning,
I started on the solitary quest
For my golden damozel, she of the yearning,
Limpid eyes, and after sundry geste
Beheld her, but with wonderment severe—
For like a serf's, those eyes mine eyes had kissed
Had boiled and burst and streaked her cheeks like tears.
Her skin, at midnight fragrant as the mist
On moonlit roses, peeled from withered flesh
Like sausage broiled.
                It was a plight
For common folk.
             I roared!
                    In all that thresh
Of vulgar pain, had not one golden knight
In pride or piety propped himself up straight
To cheer in triumph: "Honor! Country! God!"
No—the recreants hang their nameless meat
From every stump, from every wrecked facade,
And raise no praise to vindicated pride.
"Victory!" I hear my echo cry
Through leagues of thankless desert.
                      No aid,
Oh chevalier, from dry bones—no reply
From rotten lips—silence.
                   But through the night,
Soldiers with steady purpose and firm tread,
Their long-awaited victory in sight—
The golden ants are burying the dead.

KITES ON A WINDY DAY: REPLY TO A FAREWELL

Were I to tell you how I know regret—
It is like brown leaves blowing past wet
Window panes, or like torn kites in trees.

But why should we mourn losses, small or great,
Those early sketches, metaphors for all
That stings sweet into life? Let's praise the Fall
That made us brief, intact as circles, more
Than merely infinite. The play of kites
Is joy with strings attached; but let our flights
Be integral and sovereign as we soar

Above the ties our weakness clings to yet,
Secure as chains. We ride a fitful breeze
Where change is life and habit is disease.

REMEMBERING THE GREAT DEPRESSION

Summers used to be dependable:
when the neighbor boy, in the stubbornly sprouting lawn,
heaved at his mower, liff-liff-liffing through
the August crab grass, tough as tiny trees,
you knew he'd improvise a righteous sweat
halfway through the big front yard, and quit.
It wasn't guesswork, you could count on it.
Later, in a cooling Sunday gray,
as crickets tuned their chirr to the rusty pitch
of porch swings, it was an easy certainty
the next-door radio—a Gothic box
with cathedral windows and a voice
like mighty organs—would come brawling in
on six delicious stations, wobble, fade,
roar back again like fallen angels mad,
and slide away at last on a cheery voice
enchanted at a pocket full of dreams.

In spring you could depend upon the storms—
not the piddle-puddle of these degenerate days,
but loud-mouthed orgies, blistering white-on-black—
and one electric evening every spring
we knew the neighborhood would blink and dim
and suddenly go blind (it was our faith
in Order, our belief that brought the dark),
and then of course we knew in which white homes,
in which wallpapered upstairs closets, plain
ladies in lacy shawls were rummaging
like anxious ghosts, for last spring's candle ends.

In winter things were most dependable:
the water pipes, muffled like Eskimos,
always froze; cars in coverlets

coughed in the carburetor-freezing wind;
and schools—you knew they'd give up once, at least,
each year when snow filled up the streets
like breakfast bowls, and men in buckled boots
spooned at it with feeble appetites.

We were together then, islanded in the snow,
the dark, the dreams, the permanence of things:
cupboards always bare, shops on Main Street
closed, children fading into men—
men at the front door, waiting to be paid,
men at the back door, wanting to be fed—
island-people, huddled in the warmth,
dependable, the steady warmth of failure.

Summer Love and Surf

THINGS TO DO WITH RAILROADS

Once: belly-down counted the clacking cars on freight trains,
chucked roadbed stones at green glass knobs on phone poles,
smashed copper Indian-heads beneath mad engines—
those tidy histories.

Sometime: will twisted rails be
the only scribble of our past,
and learned burrowers from Mars
probe those rusty epitaphs
in search of radioactive digs,
Chicago-Crater, Boston-Gorge,
Manhattan-Chasm—shadows, once,
upon their black
negatives?

Now: in Las Vegas, Nevada,
the diesels of Union Pacific
bring clockwork sunrise to
the patchy all-night neon;
and now in Las Vegas the gray
survivors celebrate x
moments between last night's
total tidiness and
the clutter of something to come;
and now in Las Vegas the ancient
struggle flares between
barbarian plunderers riding
the random lunge of the dice
and priestesses of Order
performing methodical grinds,
precision bumps and shimmies:
these girls—their symmetry,

the rank and file of navels,
the agony of their perfection—
repeat some unremembered
agon, Makers pulsing
patterns, driving the somber
masks to moralizing
hexameters, while Xerxes
gathers up spears and marches
chaos from the eastern
sand.

Now at Las Vegas sand is skittering east,
burying pipelines, milestones, ditches; but
railroads still piece out the earth, fix
meridians along the Sands and Dunes,
far off divide the buttes of Idaho
and grid the flats of Utah, focus the
concentric desert birds, black steers on snow,
bewildered rabbits, towns—those sunset-clear
romances from a distant anarchy:
Silver Bow, Big Bend,
Laramie.

SUCCESS STORY

Shifting into low, between
purple mountain majesties
and the Valhalla Auto Graveyard,
she coughed a Chevy cough
and almost died.
On the emergency run, I noticed flags
already flopping at half-mast,
headlines huge and scared,
mobs at soup kitchens, and
through the gilded streets,
real bears pursuing speculative bulls.

Together we slid
past grave faces and white coats,
skillful fingers probing
spark gap, rocker clearance,
bore, stroke, displacement,
points, plugs, valves, rods, shocks:
the whole anatomy replaced,
atom by atom, every seven years,
fresh from fingernail to femur.
I felt old units stripped away,
factory-approved replacement parts
snugged in, threads tightened.

Coming back
we felt much better, thanks:
over amber waves of grain, Old
Glory had shinnied back up its pole,
the Dow-Jones strong and rising.
And no one was even glancing at
those skeletons in the Valhalla of
their rusting age,
who, once upon a time,
hadn't made it.

DAY OF THE HAWK

It was a sky above some antique fragment
the jet-streams feathered;
it was a time of rabbits, time of grouse,
of bells in shaded streets
where chalky-fingered girls played hopscotch and
men in cotton strolled the sidewalks, nodding.

Quick: quick as the crimson of hatred
and gorgeous as silvery death,
the hawk screamed in . . .

Under the cruelly just
heaven of antique vestiges, at last
there is no one to think it strange
that there is no one left to wonder
at the always leafless trees, the roofless homes.

TO THE GARBAGE COLLECTORS
IN BLOOMINGTON, INDIANA,
THE FIRST PICKUP OF THE NEW YEAR

(the way bed is in winter, like an aproned lap,
    like furry mittens,
    like childhood crouching under tables)
The Ninth Day of Xmas, in the morning black
outside our window: clattering cans, the whir
of a hopper, shouts, a whistle, *move on . . .*
I see them in my warm imagination
the way I'll see them later in the cold,
heaving the huge cans and running
(running!) to the next house on the street.

My vestiges of muscle stir
uneasily in their percale cocoon:
what moves those men out there, what
drives them running to the next house and the next?
Halfway back to dream, I speculate:
The Social Weal? "Let's make good old
    Bloomington a cleaner place
    to live in—right, men? *Hup, tha!*"
Healthy Competition? "Come on, boys,
    let's burn up that route today and beat those dudes
    on truck thirteen!"
Enlightened Self-Interest? "Another can,
    another dollar—don't slow down, Mac, I'm puttin'
    three kids through Princeton."
Or something else?
Terror?

A half hour later, dawn comes edging over
Clark Street: layers of color, laid out like
a flattened rainbow—red, then yellow, green,

and over that the black-and-blue of night
still hanging on. Clark Street maples wave
their silhouettes against the red, and through
the twiggy trees, I see a solid chunk
of garbage truck, and stick-figures of men,
like windup toys, tossing little cans—
and *running.*

All day they'll go like that, till dark again,
and all day, people fussing at their desks,
at hot stoves, at machines, will jettison
tin cans, bare evergreens, damp Kleenex, all
things that are Caesar's.

O garbage men,
the New Year greets you like the Old;
after this first run you too may rest
in beds like great warm aproned laps
and know that people everywhere have faith:
putting from them all things of this world,
they confidently bide your second coming.

FOUR MEASURES: EARTH, AIR, WATER, FIRE

1

Naked on the sand we are
Girdled by moralities:
The cosmic stalking of a crab,
The sea shell's vast hypotheses.
(You lie there tangible and thin;
I contemplate your skin.)

2

Clouds are counselors, too, specialists in
The impromptu—their horses forever industrious, all
Of their elephants noble, their lambs a white *Never* to sin.

3

"Behold our significance!" roar
The breakers, "how out of our mother,
The sea, we all ride to the shore,
Yet no wave is quite like another:
Diversity out of the One,
Essence give birth to Existence—
Man, take philosophy from
Our brevity and our persistence."

4

At sunset we refuse to watch the sky.
We know the strictly legal stars are waking
To march across the egoistic sea
And praise the endless glory of their making.

The sand is cold. I watch, with quiet pain,
You sheath that golden skin in jeans and sweater.
What nature skipped, we gaze into the flame
To see if blazing logs remember better.

The fire remembers only other fires,
A thousand years ago, on other beaches,
Lighting other eyes, other desires.
Be warm, and warm: is all the fire preaches.

A POEM FOR ST. VALENTINE'S DAY

Just outside our window, dawn
collapsed in the frowsy fog
and February rain won out again,
sending pigeons to cover under the noisy eaves.

In a little room
we lie awake under blankets
hugging our tented warmth until
the rain overtakes the past:
wet Saturdays at restless matinees,
wet Sundays in the timeless drone
of grandmothers and aunts,
wet summers inside steaming windows,
staring at black umbrellas in the street.

In a small room under blankets
we draw up the edges of the world
and tuck in the corners of our past:
only in our hoarded warmth can we win
the long struggle with the rain.

MIDDLE OF THE NIGHT

Mostly it is the wind
scuffing at the leaves,
but the sound
of rushing eaves

is also panic: *tick*
from the cooling furnace, *whine*
from the clock—
and someone blind

goes stumbling through the dark
of payments due, friends
lost, sick
parents, trends

in local politics,
demographic curves,
chronic aches
and pains. Bad nerves.

Someone blind is floundering in the dark
of winter edging on to blot the moon;
memories of summer noon stick
pins in his philosophy: to run

from gravity to glory is a race
with shadows. In this gloom is there a sign
from night birds, ring-tailed coons, bullfrogs, mice?
Nothing. And the December stars, Orion,

Gemini: beyond that army of
unalterable law, there is a grave

nothing. Bare in this blaze of candor, love
lies quietly and sleeps. Save
her, blindness, from your dazzling light:
her sleep is summer in the middle of the night.

SUMMER LOVE AND SURF

Morning was hesitating when
you swam at me through wave on wave
of sheet and blanket, glowing like
some dimly sighted
flora at the bottom of the sea.
Around your filmy hair, light
was seeping in with water-sounds,
low growling in the distance, like
dragons chained.

After our small storm dwindled,
we faced the rage outside, swells
humping up far out and charging in
to curl and pause
and dash themselves to soapsuds on
the stork-legged pilings of our house.
The roar was hoarser now, the wrecks of kelp
were heaping food for flies,
our long-nosed sand birds staying
close to dry land; farther out,
pelicans arched their wings in quick surprise
and gulls screamed urgently.
The call was there:
we fought the breakers out
and rode their fury back, triumphant
and again triumphant, till
at last, ears stuffed with brine and heads a-spin
like aging boxers battered,
we flopped face down on hot sand, smelling sun
and salt and steaming skin. Your eyes were suddenly

all sleep and love, there in the sun
with sea birds calling.

The sky goes metal at the end,
water, gray and hostile, lashing out
between the day and night. Plastic swans
are threatened; deck chairs, yellow towels, barbecues
stand naked to the peril, as if it were
winter come by stealth.
Still later, in the lee of dark and warmth,
we probe the ancient fear: at night
the sea is safer under glass, the crude,
wild thing half tamed to shed its past—
galleons sent to fifty fathoms, mountains
hacked to rubble, cities stripped.
At night the sea, barbaric bellows stifled,
sprawls outside the window, framed
like a dark, unruly landscape.
Behind us is a darker kind of dark:
I watch your eyes
for signals.

The music makes a pause for prophecy:
"Tomorrow, off-shore breezes and . . ."
Warmth to each other's warmth, we do not listen.

AT THE NATIVITY BAR AND POOLROOM
(Bethlehem)

Here in the cool of Christmas, shepherds drink
their partisan arak, and spit
reflectively
toward herds of infidels:
    tonight they feast on birth
    and death.

(Under the boiling rain in silent jungles,
where Buddha's love bloomed in titanic rocks,
the ravenous Shiva cut him down,
a glut of lotuses;
where Shiva sprouted stone toward heaven,
the gentle Buddha came devouring,
leaving scrub and stubble.)

In Bethlehem a neon rainbow
flashes to the earth
glad tidings:
our Father has fathered himself
and the City of God is forever!

    In a mist of arak the shepherds,
    brown men with eyes like slits,
    take the city:
    they graze among the broken stones
    of Bethlehem.
    Of Rome.

THE PATH OF RENUNCIATION
(Calcutta)

Bony bodies dry as sticks
totter on haunches, inches from earth,
caroling raptures to golden gods
for scabby lips and twisted bones,
for pale blood and milky eyes,
for flesh as gaunt as holy beef.

Contemplate this mystery:
Nirvana thrives on powdered bone.
On tins of flesh. On bottled blood.

THINKING OF NOUBLI LAROUSSI
(Algeria)

He had done for us whatever
he could do in El Oued: proudly
showed the seven palms
he owned and watered, brought my wife
dates and cool water, and
with the grave generosity
of desert people, led
us to meet his wife,
who smiled into the sand,
her schoolgirl face as
naked as the sky.

Later, cross-legged
in the blue twilight,
he spoke of his other wife,
back in Algiers, where
women walk bare-
faced through the streets—
a thought that sent a chill
prickling across the night.

The moon cupped up behind
the tips of seven palms;
we felt the distance of
horizons. "Look," he said,
speaking to our silence,
"it's very simple, really.
If you give a grain
of sand to one (he lifted
a pinch of the Sahara),

you must give a grain
to the other."

Through the level moonlight
sprinkled grains of silver
universe: simple,
really. Reno. Sodom.
Troy. A grain of sand.

Leaving for Algiers,
where women bare their faces
in the streets: "Noubli,"
I began . . .
"Ne m'oublie pas," he said,
and moon filled up his eyes
with shadows.

THREE HAIKU, TWO TANKA
(Kyoto)

CONFIDENCE
(after Bashō)

Clouds murmur darkly,
it is a blinding habit—
gazing at the moon.

TIME OF JOY
(after Buson)

Spring means plum blossoms
and spotless new kimonos
for holiday whores.

RENDEZVOUS
(after Shiki)

Once more as I wait
for you, night and icy wind
melt into cold rain.

FOR SATORI

In the spring of joy,
when even the mud chuckles,
my soul runs rabid,
snaps at its own bleeding heels,
and barks: "What is happiness?"

SOMBER GIRL

She never saw fire
from heaven or hotly fought
with God; but her eyes
smolder for Hiroshima
and the cold death of Buddha.

A WORD TO SOCRATES

"Crito, we ought to offer a cock to Asclepius."

And is death, then, old man,
the purest Idea of all,
the cure for life?

I have seen only one face
return from that gray world
you welcomed: a boy who, at
a beach beyond your strange
geography—a beach
I guarded—slipped away
and drowned. We dragged for him
in the yellowing Sunday sun
and caught him on our hook,
snagged at the elbow. His
hand broke water first
and held there for a moment,
reaching out of that clammy
death to snatch at the low
daylight—a reaching out
that caught no life but mine
who lost him.

Old man, I would not since
that hour exchange the song
of one brown bird at sunset
for the purest Idea in all
eternity.

A THOUGHT FOR SUSE POLLOK
Look not behind thee . . . lest thou be consumed.

Fall, at Auschwitz:
rain on broken brick, mist on the hills
of human hair. Stenciled luggage
calls the roll of our unsleeping past:
Gerda Singer, Leipnik;
L. Berman, Hamburg;
Joseph Sanders, Max Ullmann, Suse Pollok—
where would your beauty bloom, if in a fit
of charity your fellow citizens
had trampled out their burning patriotism?
Would you have reached Beersheba, had you not
dropped your primly labeled baggage here
and left behind your golden teeth
and splintered spectacles?

Fall: the fall brings fog,
blurring our landmarks—
which way to Auschwitz now? What star
can point the way to Haifa, Hartford,
Kharkov? In the haze
of holy causes, one gristly cord
in every human heart
strains to fire the ovens.
Look:
everywhere
the chimneys go on belching black.

LAST LINES FOR A BARITONE
Ted Haberkorn, 1893–1965

All of those songs—Dear Old Girl,
Heart of My Heart, Indiana—
are echoing there, out of hearing.

Losing our baritone,
we lost the center of things,
the heart of it all: no one else
could ride that pitch, could carry
the rest of us to music
that moved on the moving water.

At the river where we sang,
a date he pressed in the fresh
cement grows older. We,
forever the same age, watch
the gray transformations—nature
methodically emptying things:
rain trenching out his paths,
the river gouging his bank,
rust on his careful roses.

The last chords we sang together
were long ones (the banks of the Wabash,
far away   away   away)
hugging the hurt of that closeness
and resolving at last to a high
clear magic released over water,
of things never sung, never spoken:
far away   over water   away

SWEET LIFE
David K. Vest, 1919–1965

Off Malibu, like a sunny gull,
our white hull
heeled
and splashed *La Dolce Vita* from her stern
to Sunday surfers, kneeling to the sea,
to fishers on the pier,
to pink bikinis, beached. The sun
projected Catalina like a
vision. Like a promise.

When the full moon flickered out of Hollywood,
we made for harbor, but
suddenly: *fog*—
banging bells, the compass spinning,
rocks, and rasping horns!
Anchored out for hours or years,
we wallowed in the fragile hulls
of our sweet lives . . .

Now in the honesty of earth to earth,
we think *La Dolce Vita* will not sail
again: beyond the silver screen of sea,
the fog is somewhere waiting for us all.
Yet like a promise, on clear days,
we still see Catalina.

YOU SAID, THAT'S THE FOURTH BIRD THIS YEAR TO HIT OUR PICTURE WINDOW

The crash, the lightning pain, the snap
of vertebrae in neck and spine,
and one more dead. Sparrows hop
in wonder at the gods who raise
this sheet of solid sky
to murder birds.

Burying the limp thing in the rain,
I think of jangling phones at midnight,
panic, shapeless beings taking
inventory—lifetimes shrunk
to cuff links, spotted neckties,
keys, and coins.

They all say no, it's not like that,
not really; we needn't break our necks
on phony heavens. But fathers vanish,
leaving us bare against the sky,
their Last Wills always stamped
We die forever.

Ten more minutes and it's our turn,
too. Meanwhile, we keep faith
for ten more minutes. I wipe small
feathers from the killer glass
and see you inside, watching,
slightly tragic.

BUTTERWORT

Pinquicula vulgaris: flowers insectophilous,
leaves insectivorous

The bee:
"SEX is the word: feel
Out your chances, make a deal,
Procurement—then push the act
Relentlessly to an accomplished fact:
And if they tremble when you leave,
Don't let that flowery fuss make you believe
You ought to linger. They're coy, they're sweet—
But they always make ends meet.

"You youngsters wallow in remorse
At dodging stigma, using tumid force
To strip their nectar. What do you expect?
For all their fluttering, they always collect;
And they've got tricks that aren't in books:
Have you watched them hammer home their hooks
And suck away all innards, to the skin?
Look: isn't that withered wreck some of your kin?"

The poet:
Don't tell me about symbiosis; this
Is war. The younger generation's kiss
Is death to faded parents; queens exhaust
Their faithful lovers; derelict and lost,
Infants are replaced with little balls
Of filial rags. The boldest leader crawls
Discreetly up inside himself and lets
His left hand never know what the right hand gets.

Something is unbegotten, never yet
Conceived of—needed: some flowering of regret

For wastelands, something with a sense of pain
For every loss, that suffers from the rain
Falling on the unjust, knows how to rejoice
At sun in hostile countries, has a voice
That blossoms with compassion and with reason.
Can such a thing be born in this dry season?

OLD THING

is what my neighbor Mary called her cat
long before—in human terms—he got
to sixty-five and went a little stiff
in all his hingings. Much rusted now, half
the time he forgets to stalk the alley weeds
for the mice or baby rabbits he often laid
proudly at Mary's feet. On frosty nights
he creeps to where the sun comes first and sits
there, waiting, tail snugged up around his paws,
then squints into the gray sun, looking as wise
as Mary herself discussing civil rights
or war and peace or the nature of a cat.

But Mary was an even older thing
and therefore was the first to move along,
though she made it clear she didn't really hope
to find a better neighborhood. Up
to something subtly feline, Old Thing stayed
behind, looking wise and skeptical, a little proud—
looking, in fact, a bit like Mary. Watch
him now, planting each paw with the careful touch
of age; but with the eagerness of youth
sniffing at stems and slapping at snowflakes with
a sideways swipe: like Mary, he's a reproach
to any day without at least one patch
of rapture or of indignation. See
(he says with that dainty, tentative paw)
how the sun warms cats and dogs alike—isn't this
world a wonderful, disgusting place?

TOWN AND GOWN

A thousand years ago this might have been
A village crowded with the clash of bells,
The raucous laugh of rooks, the patchwork din
Of Friday fairs: a daze of decibels
Too random or too frivolous to rise
Above the lofty walls of cloisters where
The lords of intellect took exercise,
Pulling axioms from empty air.

The roars of wars and hucksters now contrive
To pierce these Gothic walls, where microscopes
And bibliographies are made to strive
To find new ways to heaven: precious hopes
Surround a gray authority who grins
At angels dancing on the heads of pins.

ENEMY

> *It is because we are in Paradise that all things*
> *harm us. When we go out from Paradise,*
> *nothing hurts, for nothing matters.*
>
> —KOMACHI

In the monstrous fact of morning,
rickshas wake with a ragged crackle,
taxis howl and twanging tongues
intone bananas in the streets.
Brash in the steaming clatter,
silence barges in,
and for a long moment I hear
the faithful rain
falling
in faithful puddles.

Somewhere
puddles are melting along a beach
while the warriors calculate:
one-average-boy-equals-one-bayonet,
a-bayonet-equals-one-boy.
Man
is the measure of all things.
And our preying guns
peer with human eyes down bunkers and mines,
across wire and water
to the enemy.

Abruptly
morning drowns the tedious water
in a hot roar.
Enemy, remember:
when the dull, rice-growing truce

explodes in brilliant victories,
when our singing shells gut your cities,
when your glory shines
in pools of our jellied blood,
and
when we are once more reduced
to peace—

nothing will harm us.
Nothing will matter.

Open Doorways

MEMO TO THE 21ST CENTURY

It was like this once: sprinklers mixed
our marigolds with someone else's phlox,
and the sidewalks under maple trees
were lacy with August shade,
and whistles called at eight and fathers walked
to work, and when they blew again,
men in tired blue shirts followed
their shadows home to grass.
That is how it was in Indiana.

Towns fingered out to country once,
where brown-eyed daisies waved a fringe on orchards
and cattle munched at clover, and
fishermen sat in rowboats and were silent,
and on gravel roads, boys and girls
stopped their cars and felt the moon and touched,
and the quiet moments ringed and focused
lakes   moon   flowers.
That is how it was
in Indiana.

But we are moving out now,
scraping the world smooth where apples blossomed,
paving it over for cars. In the spring
before the clover goes purple,
we mean to scrape the hayfield, and
next year the hickory woods:
we are pushing on, our giant diesels snarling,
and I think of you, the billions of you, wrapped
in your twenty-first century concrete,
and I want to call to you, to let you know

that if you dig down,
down past wires and pipes
and sewers and subways, you will find
a crumbly stuff called earth. Listen:
in Indiana once, things grew in it.

NOBODY DIES IN THE SPRING

Nobody dies in the spring
on the Upper West Side:
nobody dies.
On the Upper West Side
we're holding hands with strangers
on the Number 5 bus,
and we're singing the sweet
graffiti on the subway,
and kids are skipping patterns through
the bright haze of incinerators,
and beagles and poodles are making a happy
ruin of the sidewalks,
and hot-dog men are racing
their pushcarts down Riverside Drive,
and Con Ed is tearing up Broadway
from Times Square to the Bronx,
and the world is a morning miracle
of sirens and horns and jackhammers
and Baskin-Robbins' 31 kinds of litter
and sausages at Zabar's floating
overhead like blimps—oh,
it is no place for dying, not
on the Upper West Side, in springtime.

There will be a time
for the smell of burning leaves at Barnard,
for milkweed winging silky over Grant's Tomb,
for apples falling to grass in Needle Park;
but not in all this fresh new golden
smog: now there is something
breaking loose in people's chests,
something that makes butchers and bus boys
and our neighborhood narcs and muggers

go whistling in the streets—now
there is something with goat feet out there, not
waiting for the WALK light, piping
life into West End window-boxes,
pollinating weeds around
condemned residential hotels,
and prancing along at the head
of every elbowing crowd on the West Side,
singing:
Follow me—it's spring—
and nobody dies.

LAND OF COLD SUN

It is impossible not to be here
where light wells up from the river
to glow beneath the skin:
there is light here in the deep
center of things, in moments
of glittering truth.
But holding a moment in a pause
is stopping a river with your hands:
the slow smile
slowly fades,
the final word is spoken,
fingertips trail in the sand.
It is not enough
that the quick currents carry off pain,
that bitterness
swirls downstream;
because the sun goes cold,
because the touching is brief,
we are whispering
stop the river.

TEN DEFINITIONS OF LIFETIME

1

Slush, my brother said, it's
slush—the first word
I ever knew I was learning. Ankle-deep,
I shivered with cold
understanding.

2

Scout's Honor: it was another boy scout
who betrayed me—one way of finding out
what honor means.

3

At graduation, bold with endings,
I kissed her at last.
Twelve years, she said,
erasing the difference
between delay and loss.

4

When the bomb dissolved Hiroshima
every man in my company
got bombed on PX
patriotism.

5

I told the bosun:
a ship defines the ocean.
He said: horse
shit.

6
The many words for love
came easily; we would not learn the sounds
of separation.

7
In that single moment
I wanted to be immortal.
She whispered: a man who was immortal
would be as ugly
as a plastic flower.

8
All I learned in grad school
was the meaning of humility;
all I have ever forgotten
is what I learned in grad school.

9
Universe
ity: those who can, teach;
those who cannot
are the servants of teachers.

10
The poet is the unacknowledged
lexicographer of the world.

LANDING PATTERN

We give them our lives
in the fog, the men with voices
out of Midwestern computers;
arms like kites, we touch
the sinister ice on the wings, our heads
always up there, forward, brains
in the cockpit, wired
to the banks of instruments, blinking
indicators, what has gone wrong
with our lives, the red lights
chattering, what is it slipping
out of our beautiful blood,
out of the ache in our marrow,
tugging us all the way home
to treetops, houses, dogs
in friendly gardens, the homely love
of grass: squeezing our eyes to feel
the solid-state components, rock
and soil, magnetic iron
moving through our veins,
mothering elements pulling
flesh to ashes:
the gentle thump,
and they've done it again, the voices
out of Midwestern
computers, brought us in
to the promises of runways,
one more perfect landing
in our beautiful blood.

KICKING SEA URCHINS

All winter I read papers
on the train:
WORLD POPULATION UP . . .
WELFARE PROGRAM SLASHED . . .
PRESIDENT DEFIES . . .
Consistency keeps knifing
for my heart.

In June I give up surfaces—
the sea is no mere
mirror for heaven—
black-masked, we peer through safety glass
down to the clouded past, the sun
playing ripples on our vision
of yellow rocks, spiky with black
sea urchins—deeper lie the wrecks
of old caïques, and deeper still,
the rotten ribs of Roman galleys,
fat Greek argosies,
their urns of wine crusty with
snaking shells, but resin-rich,
intact—still deeper, glowing fish
stir in the dark ooze, feeding
on blind blobs half alive,
half salt, the end and the beginning:
we grope with our antennae and nuzzle
the simple cells, mothers of
our mothers.

Pulling back to sun, we rise
again to yellow rocks, black urchins.
Careless, I jam a toe into
a fellow sea-beast: brittle spines

snap off in the toe. The pain
will pulse for days, but there will be
no festering. The spines are there
to stay.
In a cold month I fold
my *Times* with care—WATER
POLLUTION RISING IN . . . Headlines
hack at my heart, but can't
cut: I feel, inside
a glossy shoe, the secret
in my toe. Can they
suspect, these others,
respectable behind
their folded papers, that I
am full of wreckage, resined
wine, the dark of a deep
and muddy past—guess
that I have become again
one part of one percent
sea urchin?

WHAT THE U.S. BUREAU OF CUSTOMS WILL CRY AT PUBLIC AUCTION ON JUNE 5

The subject, sir, cannot be made poetical.
—DR. JOHNSON

I think that when we have got used to the steam engine, we shall not think it unpoetical.
—COVENTRY PATMORE

Poet #1:

    440 Men's Wigs

    2,800 Slide Rules, Two Lots

    1 Steam Engine

    32 Bottles Russian Champagne

    500 Lbs. Oriental Hair, Assorted Lengths . . .

Poet #2:

    Oriental hair?

    500 pounds of it, in Customs?

    Customs?—listen:

    "A revolution is not a dinner party."

    "Some classes triumph, others are eliminated."

    "Political power grows out of the barrel of a gun."

Poet #1:

    500 Lbs. Oriental Hair, Assorted Lengths

    2,000 Dz. Metal Watch Bands, Four Lots

    80 Lbs. Curry Powder

    1 Steam Engine . . .

Poet #2:

    Customs?

    Just try to go home again:

    you will find

little ladies in hair nets
dragging
in silver Stingrays.
Try to escape:
your passport stamped EXIT—the belly
refuses to go.
Try to stand still:
sand
is what water does to rock.
Try to forget:
the long siege over,
the all-clear sounding pure along the walls,
veterans jam the taverns
crying April in their beer.
Oh customs, customs, the times, the manners,
500 pounds of human hair—
supervisors, superintendents, superior officers,
stay on the job:
all the common men respect
janitor work of the intellect.

Poet #1:
Also Movie Film, Bicycles, Brassware,
Perfumes, Books, Cameras,
Religious Articles, Whiskies . . .

Poet #2:
Yes:
yes steam engines,
yes firetrucks, *yes* Stingrays, *yes*
and *yes* Hondas, paddy wagons, Greyhounds,
and *yes*
prosciutto, salami, braunschweiger,
Russian champagne: *yes*, it is
the crying of kids on trikes

for bales of Oriental hair,
the crying of typists with golf bags,
of welders in silver hats—it is
the customs, the summing-up, the crying
of lots, across
chasms of inventories, range
upon range of rusting
steam engines;
it is how we buy and sell,
barter our needs,
arrange our Order,
Control:
the way we live our lives, love
our loves in the lots of lives about us,
the loves, the lives, the loves,
that happy crying.

OCTOBER SPRING

When crisp catalpa leaves
come tumbling down the frosty morning air
like tarpaulins for tulips,
it's spring again in little college towns,
October snipping at our brave beginnings,
the new year pruned away to nine lean months
of three-day weeks and fifty-
minute hours. This new year lights
no dogwood, no magnolia to find us
limping through our shrunken moments or
calling courage from our stubborn past,
the long pilgrimage of algae,
sponges, reptiles, flowers,
men. No robins linger
in the haze of this late spring
to whistle, in our fifty-minute hours,
the miracles to come: birds
of brighter plumage, richer songs,
flowers in subtler shades, men and women
walking together in peace.
But the big catalpa leaves
float crippled down the slanting sun,
brown nourishment to our long
hope, and we are clinging to
our thinning years because brown leaves
are clumsy promises: because it's
spring again.

THE PILL AND THE HUNDRED-YARD DASH

The feel of it, deep:
hairy half-humans hurtling through trees,
Cro-Magnon tracking antelope,
galloping bandits in badlands—

   sprint
the dig and pull
and heart
striding out, crying
blood to a million
years, lungs
howling the race, the race,
the furious driving thighs,
blind and sweet and
   f l o a t
on the easy coming strides and
   sprint
and the heart, the lungs, the
thighs, the throb in the tips of toes,
hot spray in the muscles
and
there, *there,*
the tug at the chest,
grateful pull of the lungs,
heart,
thighs relaxed
and

this:

that afterward
there is nothing—
only the mute
majesty
of the thing
itself.

BICENTENNIAL: THE COURSE OF EMPIRE

Looking westward: and there,
brimming over with sunrise,
the towers and magic casements
of Jersey, then
the continent itself—happy valleys,
two cars in every garage, hog
butcher to the world, pioneers,
o pioneers. That first step
beyond the Hudson stamped out
the stone age, brought empire
to the grasslands: squint,
and you can see from here
farmers on their tractors
breaking up the territories, sea
to shining sea—look again: in the Napa Valley
barefoot peasants are stomping
tubs of grapes, tribute to the emperor
standing here looking westward where
Kawasaki's roaring the Machine Age
in again by the back door, and just beyond,
small brown women are hustling
tires for Yellow Cabs, and farther on,
Greeks with torsos like marble
are casting bronze ballots for the Articles
of Confederation,
and Frenchmen are dreaming up statues
of *liberté,* and
somewhere in Spain,
caravels set sail to the unknown waters.
Empire is a curling vision: look
again, you will see
the back of your own head, looking west,
and seeing, o pioneer,
the back of your own head
looking west.

FIGHTING THE BUREAUCRACY

Have we tacked and beaten everywhere now,
run before the wind on friendly swells,
waded ashore on unknown reefs
bearing greetings, messages,
the voices of our people—only
to be fogged in here at last,
waiting?
Beyond this mush of cloud
it all goes on, the secret talks,
negotiations, flash bulbs
in the corridors; the enemy
touches official forms
with fingertips; we watch him
turn to sip coffee,
glance at the clock.
Waiting, waiting, we shuffle our feet,
jingle coins in pockets,
finger the buttons on coats—
and remember a silvery wake in the sea,
a golden doubloon of sun, dolphins
racing the foam through warm green light,
galleons standing to lee.
The long line inches forward:
fog goes sifting away like night,
and we sing at the bow of our dreams.

NEW YEAR'S RESOLUTION

Well, I did it again, bringing in
that infant Purity across the land,
welcoming Innocence with gin
in New York, waiting up
to help Chicago,
Denver, L.A., Fairbanks, Hon-
olulu—and now
the high school bands are alienating Dallas,
and girls in gold and tangerine
have lost all touch with Pasadena,
and young men with muscles and missing teeth
are dreaming of personal fouls,
and it's all beginning again, just like
those other Januaries in
instant replay.

But I've had enough
of turning to look back, the old
post-morteming of defeat:
people I loved but didn't touch,
friends I haven't seen for years,
strangers who smiled but didn't speak—failures,
failures. No,
I refuse to leave it at that, because
somewhere, off camera,
January is coming like Venus
up from the murk of December, re-
virginized, as innocent
of loss as any dawn. Resolved: this year
I'm going to break my losing streak,
I'm going to stay alert, reach out,
speak when not spoken to,

read the minds of people in the streets.
I'm going to practice every day,
stay in training, and be moderate
in all things.
All things but love.

SEEING INTO BEDROOMS

The naked eye sees only
naked flesh, lovers in their ageless
poses, the awkward elegance
of thigh on thigh: the eye
is not enough.

A 7-by-30 Tecnar
zooms to the bedside—bellies touching
call the night to witness: this
is more than a simple act, more than just
the pleasure of skin—but
something somehow foggy,
blurred.
The 8-by-40 Leitz
makes matters clearer: beads of sweat
glisten on rosy breasts—but
this thing in the glasses is no
brief seesaw of passion, these lips
on their warm adventures
to the secret places of love;
there is in it all, behind it, some
sense of loss in the act of winning,
fog in the back of the eyes.
The 10-by-50 Zeiss
trembles in the hand, the field of vision
dwindles to details of movement:
mouth on mouth, pink nipples trembling, the slow
slide of muscle and blood—pieces
of a puzzle as big as sight, still
blurred.

The last attempt: eyes
shut tight, it all comes in-

to focus—slithering shapes
of jealousy, loss, chances missed,
old loves undead—consumed
in the rhythm of hips,
spasms in thighs driving
gray chimeras out
of bedrooms, leaving the tight
mystery of love made visible
in the glaring dark
under the eyelids.

"YOUR PAPERS, PLEASE"

It always took me by surprise,
that abrupt request, blunt
as a fist: Paul Henreid, say, on a perilous
mission for the Resistance, or Charles Boyer,
off to some splendid sabotage
for Freedom—then
suddenly the flashlight, the bullying badges, and
"Vos papiers, s'il vous plaît"—and damn
if they didn't have them, every time,
passport-size, official—faked,
of course, but irresistibly
official, all
prim in their stamps
and numbers.
Nobody over here had numbers then,
or papers: astonishing, that notion
that you always carried around with you
your Identity.
Well,
the War changed all that. (You know
which war, the one where Henreid
and Boyer led us to victory, their papers
and numbers intact as armor.)
"Private Doe, 15345219, reporting, sir"—
you got used to it then, your number,
like learning your own name, your face in the mirror;
and never in your sprawling life would you ever
forget it—it was
your number.
Later we learned, They
had our numbers, too—the old
Social Security digits showing up
unexpectedly, like relatives on holidays

(Private Citizen Doe, 309-20-4763, reporting, sir)
—not just on the job,
but at school, on tax forms,
licenses, passports
(U.S. Citizen Doe, F1008541, reporting, sir)
—and somehow, before we knew it,
the numbers were there in the swivel chairs,
barking out orders, and
all of us had sort of
dwindled. Oh, we're still
around, of course, but only in practice,
not in principle: our muffled names, our shadowy
faces in mirrors have no such
authenticity
as our Blue Cross Benefit Code, 5T7W8,
or our First National Account, 22 0433 2
or even our area code, 812
or our zip code, 47401, reporting,
sir, reporting, sir.
Still, we hug
the memory of other
identities, a land where there are no papers,
where faces move through the streets
unnumbered, where we can sing
the chaotic music of catbirds,
walk the meandering streams, drift
in cumulus, shifting
from camels to weasels to whales, drink
from unmetered springs,
and taste the unweighed apples, the price-
less pears.

EAST HAMPTON: THE STRUCTURE OF SOUND

Bedrooms ease their shingles
into the yawning gardens:
the silence sucks at my eardrums
and my skull flowers open like popcorn.
Perpetual Sunday morning:
the quiet spreads out like a meadow.
I loaf and invite my soul,
and it sprawls in the shade like a toadstool.

Mondays, Manhattan is shapely
in the perfect circles of sirens,
the shrill music of taxis
making symmetries, patterns, and bounds:
jackhammers chisel my brain
to correct community standards
as the dawn comes up like thunder
out of Brooklyn, the shaper of sunrise.

TRUTH

We shall die alone.
                    —PASCAL

An army of moments:
        jade against the skin
        heavenly Aïda
        a view of Toledo
        belly and thighs—
it is always
war to the last man,
every man
is the last man,
you
are the last man
remembering
        heat and pressure
        mass and energy
        wave length and frequency
        beauty and truth—
none of your captains
will remember,
non of your non-coms
will follow you there,
only the big-eyed recruits:
        sunrise in April
        purple clowns   Beaujolais
        duckling in peaches
        rose leaves and rain—
at the final moment
they
will be with you, blindfolded
with you, standing there with
you, backs to the wall.

WESTHAMPTON CEMETERY
founded 1795

No place for elegies, in these stern
stones, bleached
by the misty light that haloes gulls
and weathers the gray shingles
of the Hamptons—no elegies, but grace:
> *Blessed are the dead*
> *which die in the Lord: my flesh*
> *will rest in hope.*

No place for elegies in this austere
devotion to joy, the faith
of the departed:
> *They do not die nor lose*
> *their mortal sympathy,*
> *nor change to us, although*
> *they change.*

No elegies for Mehitable, wife
of Enoch Jagger, died
1799 in the twenty-fifth
year of her age;
for Warren Goodall, drowned at Fire Island,
1832;
for Jennie McCue, died 1871,
aged three years, nine days—no
elegies, but grace:
> *Precious in the sight of the Lord*
> *is the death of His Saints: we sorrow not*
> *as those which have no hope.*

But for the backs that wearied out
these scars in the pale earth,
and for sailors at the aching capstans,
for fishermen scanning

the ashy sky—elegies,
yes, for all
of these—for bonneted girls
stooping till sundown in the itch
of potato fields, new widows walking their roofs
for the overdue whalers,
maids in the faded Hamptons
staring at hope chests—elegies,
chiseled in mossy stone:

> *From sorrow, toil, and pain*
> *and sin we shall be free.*

This misty light is an elegy
for the living:
bleaching our blood to water,
scaling our bone to chalk,
fading every morning song
to the minor of farewell.

SERPENT

The delicate backbone smashed,
it lived till sundown; then
its mate came for revenge.
The long muscle
glistened:
"Your eyes shall be opened,
you shall be
as gods, knowing good
and evil."
"You are no snake,"
she told him. "You
are pure superstition—go
hypnotize a bird
or suck the milk from goats. Go,
or I'll give you a backache, too."
He slithered off, limp as liver,
swearing to find some weaker time
out there in the orchard,
and the storms he would conjure then
would wreck that greenery
and stand a guard there, blazing,
with a sword.

REVISION

Why do I always see
the death in things?
Squinting in the sun, I notice
beach umbrellas sliding off,
one by one, to wet sand, waves
chopping up, full of purple tentacles,
December storms;
my cloudy look turns budding leaves to mulch,
breaks up moaning lovers,
peels the ruddy paint
from Indiana barns.

Prudence is a killing frost;
Providence poisons the soil;
Wisdom, always moving on, leaves
a brown track in the grass.

I will close my eyes and hope for
some lucky drift of jasmine,
low voices, and a dumb
trembling in the groin.

THE TENNIS PLAYER WAITS FOR
WHAT WAITS FOR THE TENNIS PLAYER

In the slippery swelter of asphalt,
in a blistering backhand return,
you wait every June, every August
for that stabbing of fate in the elbow,
that first sharp knifing of fact;
and because it comes with a certain
smug angle of the sun,
and because it comes with a bird
turning transparent as truth,
and because it comes with a cry
like preaching in the wind—
you know you are becoming
one of the pure, pale
Others; and you call back
all the grubby friends
of childhood, and command them
to surround your skin with singing.

RED KITE

Onto that long snowing of sand
the sea had nudged another derelict,
red as the rising sun in smog, and sheer
as butterflies, kite string and all,
ready to fly.
And it would have been a perfect
gift from the green tide, if
I hadn't, that day, in the idle-
ness of beaches, chucked
a stone at a silver
foraging fish—
and hit him, dead
center.
He leaped,
in a twisting flash of belly-white
so much like human pain I caught my breath
an ugly moment—then
the fish swam on, as graceful as before.
It was only that one
numbing
moment,
the terrible lifetime wait
as the fishflash in the air
meant quick or dead—how can I put it—
annihilation
hung there in the wind,
and a kite from the sea bled
red pain across the sky.

CENTRAL PARK: THE ANATOMY LESSON

The bones of the skeleton move
like levers;
muscles attach to the bones
by means of tendons, and contract
to clench fists, or deliver
a blow to the face.
When two muscles act in concert,
like the flexors and extensors of the leg
sending a knee to the groin,
it is called synergism.
The metacarpal bones of the hand
form a united mass with the bones of the wrist
and are suitable for quick
chops to the neck or kidneys.
The calcaneum, or heel bone, is the largest
bone of the tarsus; it
can in most cases crush
the thoracic cage
(notably the false or floating ribs)
in a single stomp.
Of the various bones of the skull,
the occipital, with its eggshell contour,
is the most vulnerable
to blunt objects like the tire wrench
or jack handle.

That's all for now. Repeat this lesson
till you have it
by heart.
Tomorrow night we shall consider
the circulatory system: the jugular
and other veins.

CARAVAN

It is a hazy dream, this town,
the white walls, the minarets,
the twisting cobblestone alleys:
you see yourself in the small bazaars,
haggling with wrinkled men for silk and silver,
sipping glasses of hot mint tea
in the perfume of kif and saffron.
The amazing thing is, it is true:
once upon a time you are here
among faceless women in kaftans,
old men dry as sand,
boys with the fingers of forty thieves.
But the thing you did not expect
is the eyes; these eyes were not in the dream.
They peer at you over veils
and out of the gloom of the souq:
windows of the soul, they tell you
lust, envy, gluttony, greed,
and all the homely virtues;
and the eyes you will never forget
are the milky blind eyes of children,
the charcoal rage of the woman
who hates you because you were born,
and the brown pity of that one man
who helps you when you call out.
There is no magic carpet to take you
where these eyes no longer exist;
for a thousand and one black nights
you will wake to that staggering dream.

REVOLUTION

When she came on, straight,
skin silky
black, her eyes a black
bonfire, I felt
my eyes go paler: ice-
blue,
Arctic gray—felt
my hair turn silver, skin
cellophane—
felt flesh and bone
eddying in X-rays, the air
opening up to swallow—and
I grabbed for things, the brown
table, black chairs, ebony
piano—but too
late, I had already faded into
the white shine
of the walls.

MESSAGE

> *Paris: there are pigeons, dark alleys, pale skin.*
> —CAMUS

On the windows, the windows,
this strange yellow rain,
and the soggy clock ticking: we
have defined ourselves candlesticks,
jiggers of gin
and photos and bookends and
beakers of bourbon:
      the telephone
      never   rings.

In this yellow rain, miles
are consistently one-point-six-oh-nine
kilometers long and the temperature
varies from thirty-three F
to one degree C
at twenty-nine inches of mercury falling,
and the dripping calendar
flips its pages, and yellow rain
washes away another month
      and the telephone
      never   rings.

Pigeons in dark alleys
wait for sun: we rub ourselves skin-deep
with tanning lotion and wait;
you are five-feet-five, a stately
queen of gin and I
am one-point-seven-eight meters tall
in my pale bare feet, one of the bourbon

kings, and we wait
for sun in the yellow rain
    while the telephone
    goes on never
    ringing.

MURDER

Who was it standing there
while you slept? There's
a taste on the tip of the tongue
like bitter almonds, and off
in the corner of the eye
someone is slipping into dusk
at the edge of the room, and something
without a face
is chasing you through the woods, your legs
rooted like stumps,
your screaming strangled to whimpers, and
you know in the lump of your heart
that the faceless thing
is yourself, it is
man and wife slamming doors,
in the dregs of every cup
a trace of arsenic—it is rage
at the boss, feeling
in the palm of the hand
the thump of lead pipe—it is
the fury of neighbors, the tang
of gunpowder, smell
of quicklime eating flesh; you
breathe it in with the morning
coffee, the pleasant drone
of mowing lawns,
in every blade of grass
the open razor.

You wrench yourself out of nightmare
and open your eyes
in time to see the bludgeon crashing down
and the face above it, roaring
with your laughter.

FOR LUCIA AND THE BLACK WIDOWS
OF SPERLONGA

1

They drift in whitewashed doorways, dark
shadows, tending it all: no sparrow
falls but they observe, and tally.
The village stirs under their solemn gaze:
squid and shrimp bring
flies to market, espresso
steams beneath the lone
tree
in the toy piazza,
figs and olives swell in deep July
on the slope to the shore
where men are mending nets, their big toes poking.
July is kodachrome Sperlonga: aliens
sweep across the piazza like
surf—Germans with blue-
eyed kids, Parisian mannequins squinting in blue
sunglasses, Americans in blue
jeans. They buy day-old
Le Mondes and *Herald Tribunes* and
pose in blue
bikinis on the sand, a fairy tale
of beach umbrellas.
July Sperlonga is the sweet
life that alien, Tiberius,
came for: sun, exotic fish
and flesh, orgies of blue.
September: the XXth century
retreats to Rome. Fishnet
curtains ripple in the autumn doorways,
black women on whitewash
tighten the wrinkles of their eyes

and rule again, in whispers.
The warm September Sunday Lucia walked
with Tonio to the hills and pagan grotto, dark
whispers passed along the stairstep streets,
the ashes of ancient eyes
flickered: *fallen, fallen.*

Shy creature mocked by whistles at the cafe,
by catcalls in the streets, Lucia
found no friend no priest no parent
strong as the dark old women and the whispers.
She held alone
her blackness.
In bright October sun
they found her where her farmer father kept
the poisons, her slender light
extinguished: Doctor Rinaldi
pronounced her
Pure.

As pure as Italian melodrama:
life follows art.

Dark women of villages:
in the unswept corners of the soul
are furry spiders.

2

Forty hazy winters married:
holding out again till morning chugs
with fishing boats, twinkling back
to dawn and shore and scampi-scented bed,
then setting out to mist and spray,
slapping sheets on stone at shoreside,

forty winters down and up
two hundred rocky stairsteps
jiggling tubs of sheets
on knotted hair, home to pasta brewed
in witches' kettles, floury wheels
of black bread, olive oil, the feel
of clumsy bellies,
forty winters of *ragazzi* kicking
soccer in the winding streets, of nursing
life in a treeless town to window pots,
forty winters married.

(In summer, always the aliens—
blondes in naked blue bikinis
slithering sleek bronze hips,
scorching the lounging fishermen
with heat not of Sperlonga they
brought with them to bed like panting goats
on August afternoons.)

Forty winters: parents, children dead,
shutting off the light for one full year,
patches of black across the past—
until that moonless night of logic
(what will be, will be)
when high winds tease a little boat
like kittens swatting butterflies
and *basta:*
one more widow in Sperlonga, taking
black as permanent
as brides of Jesus.
Dark women: in the tight web of Sperlonga
can anyone spin thoughts
that are not spiders?

3

Tiberius lingers in
his marble grotto, but
there are no shadows of the modern Caesar
who lost all battles, and the war.
Nazis didn't trust him to defend
even Sperlonga on its little perch
above the sea: gave the villagers one hour
to leave their whitewashed homes. They
froze for nine months
in the hills, praying *alla Vergine*
and dying *à la* Darwin, weakest first—the meek
inherit nothing from mother
nature.

A ruined bunker
three feet thick with concrete:
"7-26-44" someone has scrawled in red.
Victories came hard in these hills, every hump
took pounds of flesh—mountains, mud,
the thump of 88's,
red oozings in the rain—
but on 7-26-44
the bunker splintered at the touch
of red-eyed men.
The assault force was motley:
Americans, Brazilians, French, Moroccans
famous for two things: savagery
and rape.
When they found the Sperlonghesi in the hills,
no one escaped, the women (even
old women in black) too few—
Sperlonga is small, an army large—
the assault was universal, classic:
children, old men, everyone—the victors

violated, ravished, defiled, possessed
the villagers.
No one in these white streets
has breathed it aloud
since 7-26-44—but
before Lucia was born in Sperlonga,
there was an orgy in these hills
Tiberius would have wondered at.

And now to see a boy and girl
go hand in hand in the pagan, fruitless hills—
well,
it is no simple idyll in
the twisting stairway streets,
in the secret memories of
old women in black.

4
It is a fairy-tale village,
fit for bedtime stories: there is
a Good Lorenzo here, and a Bad Lorenzo,
a Good Milk-Lady and a Bad Milk-Lady,
a Good Beach and a Bad Beach,
and so on. The people are
charming on Sundays,
all smiles and *buon giorno*'s they walk
the extra mile with weary strangers.

"Mondays," a friend
murmurs to me in the Good Cafe in the Good Piazza
under the stare of dark women
in doorways behind fishnet screens
on balconies in windows:
"Mondays the place
is a nest of spiders. Lucia,

you know, was beaten by her father
when the whispers came, faded in her mother's
bitterness. But after the suicide
and the doctor's fact to prop their little faith,
the parents breathed indignant righteousness
and sued the woman who first
said *fallen*—just to make a fast
lira from Lucia's lonely virtue. Only
in villages," he says,
"do you find the real, the true
depravities."

"Is it fair?" I ask him. "What about
the Good Milk-Lady, the Good Lorenzo . . ."
Eyes half closed, he mutters,
"Yes. And there is a Good Church here
and a Bad Church, yes—but listen: old women kneel
by dozens in the Bad Church,
nodding while the black priests chant.
The Good Church is boarded up: that
is your fairy-tale Sperlonga.
Ciao."

He left, in a sunny evening shower
as a rainbow wrapped the village,
one end in a tomato patch,
the other in the blue shallows.
The pot of gold in tomatoes was
already known, and mortgaged; and before
the kids got down to the beach,
a sleek yacht skimmed in from nowhere good
and anchored right into the treasure.
That, my hard-nosed friend would say,
is what happens to fairy tales.

AFTERWARD

In the morning it was no better:
the chrysanthemums had frosted gray
and snow was beating the robin's nest
to splinters, in the memory
of screams.
Think
of a slash of light in lace curtains,
a solitary gnat delirious, spinning
in sun his small ecstasy—think
of the names of girls, gentle
as the melody of fountains—think
of children rubbing sleepy
eyes and stretching—think
of the flash of sea birds,
milkweed flying,
picnic tables in the shifting shade.
November wind is hissing in
apple trees run wild;
in the ruined stones of cities, boys
are boarding buses in uniform,
mothers standing
stiff in their black coats
moaning
the pain of staying alive.
Because
we never love enough,
cannot say we do,
counting the slow ticks to five o'clock, the gin
screaming like wind
in the broken flowers.

ALIVE

Uncle Jimmie had a hunch that cancer,
the rat that gnawed away behind his ears,
was part of the warm earth and silver woods
and snowy meadows in the mountains. Surgeons
stabbed at the rat: scalpels sliced away
the ears one April dawn, as catbirds,
perched in the morning treetops, mocked the calling
of cardinals. Stabbed and missed—the rat survived.
The day they clipped out Uncle Jimmie's cheeks
and upper lip, he pondered artichokes,
truffles, and a certain Tuscan wine.
And when they snipped his nose, he wept for roses
and the fresh sea breeze—and thought a while, and played
his hunch: *Stop cutting*, Jimmie told them, *let
me go to earth and snow and silver trees.*

But the rat kept gnawing, and Auntie Flo went on
reading St. Paul (*The works of the flesh are uncleanness*),
and praying, and paying the bills—and the surgeons huddled,
frowning at Jimmie's want of reverence
for faith and modern medicine. With skillful
suturing, they lifted out his tongue
and dropped the wagging muscle in a pail,
and Uncle Jim, who used to murmur quatrains
out of Omar, kept his peace. Still, his eyes
kept pleading: *Stop the cutting, let me go
to earth and silver trees!* But Jimmie knew
the rat would work in just behind his eyes,
and Auntie Flo would go on reading Paul
(*They that are Christ's have crucified the flesh*)
and praying, and paying the bills—and the pale blue eyes
would have to go: one Sunday after Angelus, Jim began
his dark forgetting of the green

wheat fields, red hills in the sun,
and how the clouds drive storms across the sea.
Some Monday following, a specialist
trimmed away one-quarter of his brain
and left no last gray memory of Omar
or snowy fields or earth or silver trees.
But Uncle Jimmie lives: the rat lies quiet now,
and tubes lead in and out of Jimmie's veins
and vents. Auntie Flo comes every day
to read to bandages the Word Made Flesh,
and pray, and pay the bills, and watch with Jimmie,
whittled down like a dry stick, but living:
the heart, in its maze of tubes, pumps on,
while catbirds mock the calling of cardinals,
artichokes grow dusty green in sunshine,
butterflies dally with the roses,
and Uncle Jimmie is no part of these.

AT THE END OF THE WORLD

Remember the quiet time
an hour before the sun, the sea
lapping silent beaches:
think of men in deerskins chipping
mussels from the yellow rocks;
think of red men camping where
rivers ran pure through pines
to the flickering sea.

Spin the globe, it's all
L.A.—freeways racing
down to Rio,
smog along the Congo, neon
screaming in Mongolia, and
Fords, eight abreast, crashing
through the Taj.

Still they are prophesying not
a quick apocalypse, only
more of the same:
Behold how the wicked flourish,
they are chanting in Nineveh,
Woe, woe to our cities
staggers the streets of Babylon.

Bittersweet lasts out the winter,
clocks tick on like gods,
a kiss is still warm on my neck,
and in a glory of guilty
joy, I hear
my own voice
singing, singing.

ON A MORNING FULL OF SUN

One of our gulls
is keening in the flat
blue light: something
is gone, is gone, is gone—a hundred
teen-age boys picked out
of mud, zipped into
plastic bags, and air-mailed
home to Mom.

White wings sweep over our beach
in formation: straw huts leap
into flame—something
is gone, is gone—
I stagger up the sand,
press my M-16
to the skull of a peasant girl,
and watch the bone
go chipping off and dancing
through the flat blue keening
air.

THE PERSISTENCE OF MEMORY

We have been through them now, the silver
anniversaries: V-E Day,
the Bomb, the wreck
of Japan, all
misted in quaintness—and still
they keep coming,
brown women swirling past,
the armies somewhere behind them, burning
the villages: always the same,
the same weary women each year,
muddy skeletons lugging
the brass pots, tugging the delicate children,
camping in culverts, eating grass—
and the rich bombers run
on their shabby targets; kids
in helmets inch
through torn jungles; somewhere at sea,
ships lob shells
at the horizon—it is all a memory
of old men:
the brave planes limping home,
balding heroes sending
their sons to glory, the bleeding
always the same, like father
like son, breastplate
and buckler rusting
in a dream of blood we
move through, open-eyed,
sons of our dreaming fathers,
waiting for all the memories
to fade.

PEACE WITH HONOR

Solitudinem faciunt, pacem appellant.

1

The outer provinces are never secure:
our Legions hold the camps, their orders
do not embrace the minds
and hearts of barbarians. So, when the late-
late news reported the outlandish
screams in that distant temple,
the great bronze Victory toppled,
red stains in the sea, corpses
stranded by the ebb tide—all of that,
and only four hundred
armed men at the garrison—why,
of course it had to come, the massacre,
the plundering.

2

It was the decade's scandal at home,
the humiliation, the Eagles gone.
Senators put on grim faces
and gossiped over bloody
Marys—what laureled head would roll for this?
Reports from the field
were cabled not to the Emperor but
to the Joint Chiefs, to filter
through at last, edited
and heavy with conclusions: the traitor,
they revealed, was not in uniform,
the treason was our own permissiveness;
in sterner times our Fathers would not
have suffered such dishonor.
We nodded: yes, they knew,

the Chiefs, what ancient virtue was.
The twilight shudders of matrons
seasoned our resolution. Somber, we took
a fourth martini, wandered to the couches,
the tables rich with peacocks' tongues,
and nodded,
nodded, waiting.

3

They sent our toughest
veterans, the Ninth Legion, the Fourteenth,
the Hundred-and-First, their orders un-
ambiguous: teach the barbarians respect.
Our marshals chose the spot: a steep defile
covering the rear, our regular troops drawn close,
light-armed auxiliaries at their flanks,
cavalry massed on the wings.
The enemy seethed everywhere, like a field
of wind-blown grasses.
There were the usual
harangues, the native leaders boasting
their vast numbers, screaming
freedom or death;
our generals, with that subtle sneer
they learn at the Academy,
pointing only to the Eagles on their tall shafts—
and every man remembered
the shame of Eagles fallen, comrades' bones
unburied: there was that curious thing,
men in bronze and steel, weeping.
And then the charge, the clash of arms,
cavalry with lances fixed, the glorious
victory: a hundred thousand tons of TNT
vaporized their villages, their forests were

defoliated, farmland poisoned forever,
the ditches full of screaming children,
target-practice for our infantry.
The land, once green and graceful,
running with pleasant streams in the rich brown earth,
was charred and gutted—not even a bird
would sing there again.

4
A glorious victory, of course,
but in a larger sense, a mandatory act
of justice: the general peace
was kept, the larger order held; peasants
for a thousand leagues around
are working their mules again.
Our prisoners and Eagles all returned,
we dine at the rich tables,
thinking of the Sunday games,
thinking of anything but rebellion—thinking
the honor of Empire
is saved.

WAITING FOR THE FIRE

Not just the temples, lifting
lotuses out of the tangled trees,
not the moon on cool canals,
the profound smell of the paddies,
evening fires in open doorways,
fish and rice the perfect end of wisdom;
but the small bones, the grace, the voices like
clay bells in the wind, all wasted.
If we ever thought of the wreckage
of our unnatural acts,
we would never sleep again
without dreaming a rain of fire:
somewhere God is bargaining for Sodom,
a few good men could save the city; but
in that dirty corner of the mind
we call the soul
the only wash that purifies is tears,
and after all our body counts,
our rape, our mutilations,
nobody here is crying; people who would weep
at the death of a dog
stroll these unburned streets dry-eyed.
But forgetfulness will never walk
with innocence; we save our faces
at the risk of our lives, needing
the wisdom of losses, the gift of despair,
or we could kill again.
Somewhere God is haggling over Sodom:
for the sake of ten good people
I will spare the land.
Where are those volunteers
to hold back the fire? Look:
when the moon rises over the sea,
no matter where you stand
the path of the light comes to you.

LOVE POEM

The lonely pull of blood
at midnight: capillaries
seeping slow in firm
flesh—a closed system.

Touching: the thrill of cool
skin, sing-song of
her breath, the gurgle
of many yards of tubing
somewhere deep, and
always the thump, thump
of her tough heart.

ARS POETICA

Think of it, nine thousand
breakfasts together, and now
coffee again for the first time: what
a virginal movement it is, this
silvering together, every day
the very first day, every night
the first night, not a film replayed, more
like pages in a long book, strata
in these limestone hills we live in,
two billion years old.
We're not yet as old as the limestone,
but we're catching up—or rather,
reducing the proportion, like a kid brother
gaining on his elders; we're gaining
on the limestone and
beginning to see
it's an art, like Cellini's, this
silvering—like poetry, reminding us
in its earnest, nagging way,
that every new minute we risk
immortality, surviving
for nine thousand days by luck or cunning;
but at the end we're sent to press
with all our typos intact, fossils, captive
in the ancient rock. Meanwhile,
we're all such fumblers, gauche,
all thumbs: maybe
poems and marriages deal
mostly in failures—on the way to shape,
nine thousand blemishes hitching a ride. Maybe
only a poem or a silver bowl
will tell us as well as love: that

these are the only raw
materials we have—the painful
moments of wonder,
the small, well-meant betrayals, rain
in the limestone hills.
Well, we're not finished yet;
the revisions are still in process, a line here,
a day there, the whole thing
taking on a kind of polished
mutilation, a scarred silver florin,
a weathered hill,
an epic fragment.
There's time yet to get it—not right,
of course, but anyway revised,
emended, more mature
in its lumpy way. Think of it,
two billion years of shaping:
it's a beginning.

THE GIRL WHO HATED THREES

At the beach
she always took my hand
as though we were sophomores again,
or as though a wave might race in like
some wild Greek myth
and sweep her out to sea—
but of course it wasn't that;
she took my hand
to pair the two of us off
against the world. She hated threes,
didn't believe in the Trinity,
wouldn't read trilogies or listen to trios
or type in triplicate.

But all that came to me late,
late one winey evening,
with a Burgundy sun going down
and a Rhinish full moon rising,
came to me in that swimming twilight, as
she took my hand again:
that the rhythm of love is always
a pulsing of two's—and in
the dawn of that twilight vision,
the reeling gulls paired off, crabs
staggered the sand all twinned,
and a brace of boozy bluefish
leaped and carried on
as her stubborn grip held
wax and wane,
ebb and flood—and all the beautiful
barbarians drifting on that twilight beach
paired off in a tug

of give and take,
lose and hold—
and the summer tides went on in the image of love:
in and out,
in and out.

SAVIOR

It is a troll's morning with bells,
chimes of Black Mass under my eyelids,
every morning my body found
floating in formaldehyde, bearing
bruises that don't show,
the trolls clubbing me all night,
smashing nerves;
a shadow of myself comes
at me, whiskered, eyes
pickled in brine, mouth a swamp
of last night's beer, the sun
stuck somewhere in clouds, everything
outside gray, the grass dead as a mummy—
even the ground is dirty,
dusted with road salt, nothing will ever
live in it again.
I hear you roll over in bed, and feel
a twinge of something
one part felicity, one part despair—
out there in the gray, the single ones,
bachelors, widows,
teen-age kids delirious
with lust and loneliness, how
do they make it through
the bludgeoning of March?
Bedsprings hail your rising.
I know your yawn, the rubbing
of eyes, feel you
warm along my withered skin—am I
saved?
We gaze at troll's dawn together, and
the first robin
flutters in to whet his beak on twigs;
his mate, clutching the filthy earth,
listens to the black black bells.

HEART OF STONE

In May, the pressure on
the temples, toes: I keep
my hat on at work, in shops, at bars;
my shoes come loose and shuffle.
June: I drop disguises in
the sun, horns and hooves agleam,
kicking sand.

On an azure coast,
browning like good French bread,
we pick up pebbles on the beach.
She bends, showing white skin under
her bikini: my goat blood races.
"Look!"
It's special: red, a heart
so perfect she's sure it's carved.
Carved? By whom? And is it an old
stone, I wonder. "All stones are old,"
she murmurs in the naked wisdom
of nymphs: "It's a message."

I feel the menace tingling
in my horns.

Snorting in midnight lechery,
I fall away from the moment:
who carved the thing, red, perfect?
Some other split-hooved creature, in last
summer's sun?—the sea
has smoothed at it much longer. A monk,
then, in the dark time, praising
his long frustration to heaven? Or
maybe some passionate Goth, bleeding

guilt for a past in ruins?
This is graveyard soil; below
our seesaw bed the rocks
of Roman walls are still
intact—"All stones are old."
Well, Roman, then, my lusty
nymph, the heart of a
centurion, a slave?
I wrench at time, and cherish
skin to skin. We sleep.

In the milky light I am
already wide-eyed, wondering:
perhaps, perhaps
some tanned old Greek, tired
of getting and spending, a token for
his charming native boy? Or—
the coarse hair bristles on my spine—
Cro-Magnon himself (all stones are old)
carving his red delight
in the misty morning of man-hood?

Stop! My horns ache
with reflection—our breed is not
accustomed . . . I feel itching
in my hooves, glance at her browning
skin, stirring with easy
breathing, feel my roots
atingle, reach out
to her white breast—but
think. Think. Think again—
and steal off, click-click of hooves
on tile, to stand on pebbles,
wondering: who sent
this memory to fog
the sunny morning?

BIRTHDAY CARD TO MY MOTHER

The toughness indoor people have:
        the will
to brave confusion in
mohair sofas, crocheted doilies—challenging
in every tidy corner some
bit of the outdoor drift and sag;
        the tenacity
in forty quarts of cherries up for winter,
gallon churns of sherbet at
family reunions,
fifty thousand suppers cleared away;
        the tempering
of rent-men at the front door, hanging on,
light bills overdue,
sons off to war or buried, daughters
taking on the names of strangers.
You have come through
the years of wheelchairs, loneliness—
a generation of pain
knotting the joints like ancient apple trees;
you always knew
this was no world to be weak in:
where best friends wither to old
phone numbers in far-off towns;
where the sting of children is always
sharper than serpents' teeth; where
love itself goes shifting
and slipping away to shadows.
You have survived it all,
come through wreckage and triumph hard
at the center but spreading
gentleness around you—nowhere
by your bright hearth has the dust

of bitterness lain unswept;
today, thinking back, thinking ahead
to other birthdays, I
lean upon your courage
and sign this card, as always,
with love.

CONGENIAL POET DESIRES INTENSE
RELATIONSHIP WITH WARM, INTELLIGENT POEM

In the city, summer
slugs us like a bursting pillow;
feathers whisper
down our itching necks:
SENSITIVE, LITERATE PROFESSIONAL MAN
SEEKS ATTRACTIVE NON-CONFORMIST GIRL . . .
The long streets
sizzle
like hibachis; fans all over town
begin to whisper,
calling for help in every bus and subway:
GAY MALE, 25, SLIM, HANDSOME,
WANTS GOOD-LOOKING, ATHLETIC MAN IN 20'S . . .
We hold hot hands crosstown;
why is the girl in blue tennis shoes pouting,
the woman in the back of the bus
humming to someone:
PRETTY, TRAVELED DIVORCEE, YOUTHFUL 50'S,
SEEKS DISCRIMINATING, MATURE MAN
FOR INTELLECTUAL STIMULATION IN DAYTIME,
EMOTIONAL COMMITMENT AT NIGHT . . .
In this city
there is never night,
our eyelids
will not work, we sleep
watching our lives flicker
on the walls, feeling the heat close in,
hearing the whispers
rustle in the brilliant midnight parks:
MALE, 29, ENJOYS MUSIC, TENNIS
DESIRES VIGOROUS, REFINED WOMAN
FOR OUTDOOR SPORTS AND BACH . . .

CULTURED, PETITE WIDOW. GOOD DISPOSITION,
WANTS MEANINGFUL RELATIONSHIP
WITH BALANCED, CREATIVE MAN OVER 30 . . .
HEALTHY, WELL-TO-DO BACHELOR
SEEKS EROTIC LIAISON
WITH SENSUAL FREE SPIRIT . . .
In this city the whispers
roar at us:
Where there is no silence
can there be speech?
Where there is no darkness
can there be light?
In a burden of heat
can there be warmth?
In the crush of bodies
can there be feeling?

We listen
to the whispers in the air
and feel the terrible
compassion
come on like summer rain.

THIS MOMENT

Wasn't it only a day or two ago
birches were beginning to yellow—and now
rain streaks the windows and soaks
the trophies of our summer's labor, geodes,
shells, marigolds. Wet
tiles are working loose
and roofs are leaking autumn
as your touching finds again
the pity of people on subways, at public parks
in their brave summer dresses, finds
the land of inside-out: in the bedroom
your sun comes up again,
in the kitchen your nearness
turns water to wine, a telling of moments
clairvoyant as geodes,
outside plain as pudding,
inside jewels. Treasures shine
in your dazzling skin:
the shape of pears, gold
of nectarines, all
symmetries, and words
like melody, intelligence, waking, sleep.
To all the seductions of stone
you offer the gift of moments:
shadowy, hard,
immortal.

FIRST SNOW

After the long red warning of maples
it is still a surprise attack, the hordes
sweeping in at night, and at dawn
riding the shadows
        as we lie in the shelter of blankets,
        in the summer blood of our loving,
        and feel the old terror of time
        freezing the land.

The outer walls are abandoned,
the same every year, the flowers
frozen; we dig in behind the storm windows,
remembering noon in the hazy
shimmer of cornfields,
remembering noon with aspens
and faraway bells—
but each year the losses: the old ones,
limping off to their dim consummation,
tell us fear is a small brown mouse
come in from the cold to chew
at the belly nerves,
and it touches us now, the truth
of the whole gray assault: it is war
to the ultimate cold
        and we lie in the shelter of blankets,
        in the summer blood of our loving,
        and feel the old terror of time
        freezing the land.

IF MARTHA IS A MODEL MOTHER-IN-LAW, SHE IS DEFINITELY THE LATEST MODEL

> *But Martha was cumbered about*
> *with much serving . . .*
>
> —LUKE 10:40

They move in the sunshine of caring,
these women whose names are never
Dulcinea or Rosalind, not even Mary,
these women in sensible shoes
whose names are always Martha:
they pad through a quilted landscape
of Bibles and potted ferns,
the tinny piano in the parlor
playing rag and Rock
of Ages to the milkman's immortal horse,
and Martha is always there, singing
lullabies to the children
and mending checkered trousers
and putting on the kettle—
and things go on like that, as if
the potted ferns were paper and
the sun were embroidered onto a muslin sky,
until this particular Martha,
come from a childhood earlier than airplanes,
young with the brand-new Model T
and the women's vote, a lacy bride,
younger as Lindy hopped to Paris,
younger still with VJ Day
and men on the moon and rockets
to Mars, a lacy bride
for forty-five summers, then
watering grave chrysanthemums
on Sunday afternoons forever; after

seventy winters of starched white shirts
and ovens and diapers and needles
and pins, needles and pins, bright
with the sunshine of caring,
she's traded the horsehair loveseat in
on an air-conditioned Buick,
and her special daiquiris have come
a long way from lemon-
ade in the shade; she's not
looking back, this Martha, she's
holding a handful of aces, playing
dealer's choice with life.
And she isn't missing a trick.

ECONOMICS

These are the iron laws of love:
    nothing ever comes free;
    there is no such thing as a bargain;
and   *you never get more than you pay*
    and pay
    and pay for.
Blue letters in the bottom drawer:
profit and loss. And in bed
the expensive breathing,
the steadiness a faithful
whisper:
    never sell out,
    never sell out.

IN TWO DEGREES OF COLD

That afternoon, you snapped a sprig
of forsythia,
put it in a glass to warm and flower.
I knew it wouldn't; winter was
too deep.

In the morning, snow came, delicate,
big flakes floating like
kids' paper cutouts; all day
the neighbors' doorways twinkled
green and red, running lights in snow.
At dusk the flakes got smaller,
businesslike, stuck
to the sides of things. Somewhere
wheels whined in the dark. The snowplow
blinked in bedroom curtains.
We shivered at far edges of the blanket.

By morning we were adrift,
boot-deep in fluff
still coming—shoveling to the street,
cursing the snowplow's ridges.
All day it whistled, even in noon thaw,
icicles dribbling from eaves.
We stayed inside, made coffee, silently
passed the papers, watched the weather
on TV, glanced across the long room at each
other, pacing,
wiped steam from windows, shoveled for the mailman,
the paper girl.
And waited.
By night the snow was wetter, finally
almost rain, freezing
where it splashed: ice and water

had forgotten which was which. In bed
we heard icicles ticking lower,
the sander rumbling past.
We burrowed into blankets
separate
and would not sleep.

It never went quite dark.
When morning lightened the white
night, the world was ice
from eaves to evergreens, houses made cages
of icicles, snow crusted
crystal-hard, to bear the weight
of kids and dogs, stiff-legged on the glare;
bushes sagged with the burden,
birches drooped, and already snow
had started piling up on ice,
the sky gone crazy, dumping the stuff
just to get rid of it, a sifted
avalanche.

The sun forgot us. Day and night
the sky was a wicked gray on gray, and always
the swirl
of feathers in the air.
Outside nothing moved:
dogs stayed in, the rabbit tracks
stopped, birds
lined the neighbor's chimney
and didn't stir.
The furnace clicked on, whirred.
We toyed with coffee, watched
each other, nervous,
holding out for thaw.

One morning, in a glass:
yellow flowers.

A KIND OF FRUITFULNESS

The apple tree
is pregnant again: at ten o'clock
the sun is lighting torches
in the blossoms, in the breasts
of nesting robins—it is on us
again, the season of
beginnings; we know where it leads, the way
from a vision of toys to the fact
of thinning hair. Not
youth, not freshness, then,
not innocence: we have had
that music, know
its endings. Apple tree,
love your blossoms; but we
stand outside fertility,
trusting the gift of living:
ripeness, ripeness.

BETTER HALF

You are witching time and space,
my love,
in your race to the one o'clock plane,
the eight o'clock curtain,
calling to every fickle moment,
Linger awhile;
your dependable tardiness
is a way of wringing life
to its last hope, promising
a moratorium on death—because,
my love,
if you should die,
everything in the world would stop:
planes would sit forever
on weedy runways,
actors would pause
forever in rehearsals . . .
But of course you will not die:
you'll go on scurrying through space,
constantly making up time,
knowing we are better late
than forever.

LOVE IN THE RAIN

In the primitive green of midnight
it is weather for ducks: mallards
are swimming through clover, teals
wading in crabgrass;

> *our thighs are as slippery as grass,*
> *dandelions tickle our rubbery*
> *backs as we roll, summer*
> *stalks through the rain in our fingers;*

herons stalk the deep grass
stabbing for minnows, swans
are cruising the garden, sandpipers
sway through sand;

> *the sky sways with the rain,*
> *wavering shapes of trees*
> *show us the wind: in the drizzle*
> *our skin is a jungle fever;*

it's a jungle out here, frogs
one jump ahead of the cranes,
worms waiting for cranes
in the hungry earth;

> *our bodies are stalking the earth*
> *as we sway through a jungle of grass,*
> *feeling inside us the rain*
> *as it comes and it comes and it comes.*

SCRAPBOOK

What I remember is
    the overhead fan in Bangkok,
    turning like wheels in old movies,
    slowly backwards;
I remember
    turning to you and squinting
    as if you were shining on me.
What I remember is
    evening haze in Calcutta,
    dung firing the brass pots;
I remember
    your blondness in brown
    children: strange foreign light.
I remember
    the blind camel at Isfahan
    plodding in circles, grinding the bloody husks
    of pomegranates; and
    in the empty bazaar
    your slow step in the dark.

Do you remember
    the parting in Trieste, sunset
    slipping through bars in the station, the train
    clanging like doors of dungeons;
    and pain splitting the night
    like summer lightning?
What I remember is
    glances that looked deep,
    the touch of skin that felt bone,
    whispers out of the telling
    of the heart.
Do you remember

in the quays and airports of our past,
that fading Schedule of Departures,
our belonging only to places, things—
adrift
inside our permanence?

Darwin's Ark

. . .

PREFACE

*I think that a man who wants to write in the
twentieth century makes a great mistake if he
doesn't begin by reading* The Origin of Species.

—BASIL BUNTING

I consider myself lucky, as a poet, to have been interested in
Charles Darwin all my adult life; but that had nothing to do with
my schooling. As it turned out, it was (in a Shandean way) rele-
vant to my experience of Darwin that I was conceived in the
same month that John Thomas Scopes was arrested and
indicted by a grand jury for the crime of teaching evolution to
the schoolchildren of Dayton, Tennessee, and that in due course
I was born in the same month that the legislature of the state of
Mississippi duplicated the Tennessee anti-evolution law. My
memory of those events is imperfect, but I conjure up the
temper of the times from the historical fact that, in the year of
my birth, the famous evangelist Aimee Semple McPherson,
concocting an alibi for an extended rendezvous with her lover,
claimed to have been kidnapped by gamblers, dope peddlers,
and evolutionists; and from the establishment, a year after my
birth, of the American Anti-Evolution Association, an organi-
zation open to all citizens *except* "Negroes, Atheists, Infidels,
Agnostics, Evolutionists, and habitual drunkards."

So by the time I started school, it was not surprising that the
anti-evolutionary laws had spread to Arkansas and Florida, that
there had been agitation for similar laws all around the country,
and that high-school and college teachers had been fired for
mentioning evolution in the classroom. By the time I learned
to read, textbook publishers had already got the message. The
word "evolution" and the name of Darwin had been deleted
from virtually all public-school textbooks, and continued to be
banned, partly by law and partly by self-censorship, for four
decades. The public schools of my Hoosier home town were no
different from most others in America: in twelve years of educa-
tion, including a high-school course in biology, I never heard

the name of Charles Robert Darwin. Across the nation, the invisible government of church fathers and school boards had in effect abolished a natural law from the schools. It was, in retrospect, a rather astonishing feat, the educational equivalent of, say, the Flat Earth Society abolishing gravitation. So my fifty-eight classmates and I, like many thousands of our contemporaries around the country, graduated from high school totally ignorant of one of the most basic facts of life: the perpetual functioning of organic evolution.

(It would be gratifying if all that were now changed, but alas, recent studies indicate that even today evolution is ignored in many American high-school biology courses.)

Almost by accident, I finally did get around to reading *The Origin of Species*, which I had packed in my sea bag for a long trip in the merchant marine. I was the same age then as Darwin was when he set out on the *Beagle*, and because of his book, my trip, too, was a voyage of discovery. In 1948, before the paperback revolution, the only cheap and easily available editions of the classics of literature, science, and philosophy were the Everyman and Modern Library editions. Fortunately, there was a Modern Library "Giant" with *The Origin of Species* and *The Descent of Man* in one volume: exactly one thousand pages of small print. I still have the book, a bit dog-eared from thirty-five years of travel and use, and much underscored with the smudgy blue first-generation ball-point pens I carried to sea.

I read that book in noisy mess rooms, surrounded by cribbage-playing seamen. I read it in my bunk at night, the persistent bedlamp sometimes annoying my watchmates. I read it on deck in the sunny waters of the Mediterranean, meanwhile collecting extra hazard pay because stray floating mines from World War II were still sinking ships there. The 1948 marginalia reinforce my memory of being interested in the mechanisms of natural selection, but the more detailed marginalia indicate that what most held my attention, in both *The Origin* and *The Descent*, was the information bearing upon the relation of human beings to the rest of nature, and the philosophical implications of evolution.

I am sure it is difficult for anyone reared in a more enlightened time and place to imagine the sense of exhilaration in a young person schooled in Midwestern fundamentalism, reading Darwin and understanding evolution for the very first time. But I recall that experience vividly: the overwhelming sanity that emerged from Darwin's clearly thought out and clearly written propositions; the relief at being finally released from a constrained allegiance to the incredible creation myths of Genesis; the profound satisfaction in knowing that one is truly and altogether a part of nature.

I couldn't have foreseen it at the time, but I have been reading Darwin ever since—*The Voyage of the* Beagle, *The Expression of the Emotions in Man and Animals,* the books on barnacles, on earthworms, and on orchids, the journals, the notebooks, the autobiography—that whole prodigious Victorian labor of love. And I have been writing about Darwin ever since: a doctoral dissertation, an abridged edition of *The Origin,* articles, lectures, chapters, reviews, the Norton Critical Edition, *Darwin*—and many poems.

Darwin was inspired with the idea of natural selection by reading Malthus; I was led to Malthus by reading Darwin, and became so concerned with overpopulation as to write a book about it, called *The Silent Explosion,* and to edit the Norton Critical Edition on Malthus. Many of the poems in this volume have their conceptual and emotional roots in the deplorably neglected problem of overpopulation. The continued proliferation of human bodies and human needs, with the resulting competition for limited resources, destruction of natural habitats, growing pollution of the environment, endangering of other species, even the threat of extinction itself: all of these are ultimately Malthusian as well as Darwinian themes, and they stir beneath the surface of many of these poems . . .

P. A.
Bloomington, Indiana
April, 1984

THE SKELETONS OF DREAMS

He found giants
in the earth: Mastodon,
Mylodon, thigh bones
like tree trunks, Megatherium, skulls
big as boulders—once,
in this savage country, treetops
trembled at their passing.
But their passing was silent as snails,
silent as rabbits: nothing at all recorded
the day when the last of them came
crashing through creepers and ferns,
shaking the earth a final time,
leaving behind them crickets,
monkeys, and mice.
For think: at last it is nothing
to be a giant—the dream
of an ending haunts tortoise and Toxodon,
troubles the sleep of the woodchuck
and the bear.

Back home in his English garden,
Darwin paused in his pacing,
writing it down in italics
in the book at the back of his mind:
> *When a species has vanished*
> *from the face of the earth,*
> *the same form never reappears . . .*
So after our millions of years
of inventing a thumb and a cortex,
and after the long pain
of writing our clumsy epic,
we know we are mortal as mammoths,

we know the last lines of our poem.
And somewhere in curving space
beyond our constellations,
nebulae burn in their universal law:
nothing out there ever knew
that on one sky-blue planet
we dreamed that terrible dream.
Blazing along through black nothing
to nowhere at all, Mastodons of heaven,
the stars do not need our small ruin.

NOSTALGIE DE LA BOUE

1

Out there in the cornfields, we knew
about mud, its personalities
as shifty as the snow
Eskimos have a dozen names for—
the muck in onionland, sponge
rubber of pastures, clay
that mooshed into guck to yank
your boots off—so full
of dormant seeds you could smell
in every squish of it
the brooding life: that
was mud you could call mud, not
this sissy sterile city stuff
in gutters and vacant lots.
In the little town I lived in, mud
was everywhere in April, when the snow
has taken final leave, but the grass
doesn't believe it, and big bare
patches in the lawn that in August were
triumphant crabgrass
are swamps of maple twigs, bark, debris
of winter, waiting to be earth,
and the hairless denizens of this land,
suspicious of heaven, wear
their sheepskins tight, knowing
that any minute the sky could fall,
shattering spring—and yet
they smell it, too, the promises:
perfume of mud in April,
all around us,
waiting.

2

We go back a long time together,
Hoosiers and mud: to devil summers
on Noble County farms, and weariness
no city work ever shared
with a back, the ache in our marrow dissolving
to memories of mosses, ferns,
protozoans in the soup
of ancestral mud: all
in our bones, out there in that little town
that looks like a game of tic-tac-toe
run wild, right-angle streets,
proud of their civilization, superimposed
on the Indiana Territory, contours
trod upon by deerskin moccasins
come on the lost land-bridges:
brittle streets laid over first
with gravel, then with bricks,
concrete, asphalt—generations
of style, paving over the mud;
there, in that formal
web, in April, forsythia
surprised the mud with prophecy
of dandelions, firecrackers,
hopscotch shade of maple trees, croquet balls
lumping along a rough back yard
toward the tragedy of
chrysanthemums.

3

They say build your houses on rock,
but in Noble County we built
on mud, and in April
a boy could stand on a white front porch,

lacy with spindles and railings,
and stare at the mud
and think about summer and a girl
in a window a mile away,
looking out at the mud, thinking
about a boy on a white front porch,
and a mile of wet earth
between them, as full of life
as the mud that bore flatworms and slugs,
the first amphibians, pioneers,
lizards and lemurs, and finally
upright silhouettes loping across
the mothering mud—on quiet nights,
as arrowheads bloomed in the dark of the moon,
we felt it all, and you
can feel it, too, closing your eyes,
holding your wrist, feeling the jellyfish
tugging the pulses: *there*
and *there.*

4

It was our birthright in Noble County, that
ancient ground, the farmers always
cursing the mud
but coaxing the tractors through it
somehow, spring plowing turning up
ten thousand years of spearheads—then
the Saturday trips to town, to buy
clodhopper shoes at Penney's
and popcorn at the old red wagon, and sit
in Chevies parked at the curb,
loose jaws munching the salty corn,
watching the *Homo sapiens* strolling Main Street,
clutching their mates by the forearm, guarding

their young at their sides, waiting
for sun, and Sunday School, and the tail-
less primate with opposable thumbs
gripping his black book, baying
at sin, as April sun pours
purple through scenes of Creation, slanting
on pews of leathery muzzles and snouts;
and the fields of Indiana mud
go on unplowed, tractors waiting
for godless Monday, spring-
tooth harrows suspended in time,
and lawns that would soon be grass
for badminton, still mud,
and flagpoles all over town
rooted in mud, flowering stars
and stripes forever, and
on one white porch,
an accident of molecules
and history, looking like
a young boy standing in Sunday spring,
expectantly, as if
he could walk a mile
through mud, and speak to the girl
in the window—as if he could
step off that white porch into feelings
he will never have; but the house,
built on mud, will nevertheless
survive the boy and the girl; and this one
silent moment,
promising grass and the cool shade
of maples, is still out there
on a front porch
waiting.

STATE OF NATURE

1

This is how it's done: the queen
of beasts, prima donna, hunching
in dry grass, is perfectly
dry-grass, her contours
miming the landscape. Some
suns ago there had been
the zebra, before that the eland;
memories of feasting stir
through her veins, the call in the belly
like drumming hooves of antelope.
Muzzles nudging the soft shoots:
the old drama
begins again; her yellow eyes squint
like a kitten petted; her nose
twitches in the downwind tang—
the sudden bound: gazelles
stampede across the veldt, Keystone
Kops zig-
zagging in speeded-up film, until
the herd
strings
out,
tropical crack-the-whip, the weakest
tiring, fear in the breath,
death in the watery legs.
One pair of antlers falls
behind; now
the cat knows the shape of her dinner:
the beautiful Pavlova
leap, the final hug and kiss,
claws into flanks, jaws
in the spinal cord, and

the gazelle is fresh meat only.
Tableau: to the right
a blurring of dust, survival
of the fittest; in the foreground
the queen of beasts, prima donna, panting
hugely.
She buries her head
in the warm belly; blood
illuminates the grass. Sweetbreads
and tripe, the best parts first,
then the shredding
of muscle from bone: the thighs,
the pectorals—finally
sculpture, the graceful
leg bones unveiled, rib cage
exhibited.
Casually, like a tabby
turning away from a bowl, the queen
lumbers to the flickering banyan shade,
makes herself comfortable as a sphinx,
head on paws, and sleeps. The scene
gathers pace, no longer a two-
character drama. Seedy extras,
waiting in the wings,
pick up their cues: hyenas,
drooling through all that gormandizing,
clown their way to center
and rake off strips of flesh;
vultures drop out of the sky
like tent flaps in a gale,
upstaging the barking hyenas,
and beak into bones: the skeleton
goes bare, instant fossil. Evening
whimpers across the veldt; in minutes
dark drops in, the vultures exit;

little creeping things come out
and nibble at leftovers, mousy
silhouettes, getting
in each other's way, Marx
brothers in a panic; and
the immortal cockroach,
under a kleig-light moon,
shuffles through her late
late show.

2

This is how it's done: at Tierra del Fuego
we stalk the coast, naked as Spirits—we
are the great hunters, rocks
and slings ready for blood. When
the Spirits are kind to us, floating
a dead whale into shore, we hack at it
with sharp stones, delicious
rancid blubber, feasting
till our bellies bulge; make
ponchos out of the blubber,
holes for our heads, and nibble
the edges slowly, our deepest bones
feeling the twilight of
no lucky whales, no seals.
On easy days, we send the women
to dive for sea-eggs, or bait
the small fish in the bay; we streak
our faces white with clay
to please the Spirits: these
are the good times.
But the sins of wicked people,
wasters of food,
bring the screaming winds; then
the hungry nights come on.

We lie in ambush: if
we can trap the evil
tribesmen to the sunrise,
the feeding on their soft parts
will be sacred; but
if we cannot, there are still
the old women.
They feel it coming:
when babies are squalling for milk
and young breasts have gone dry
and bellies are snarling like curs,
they know it's coming,
the old women:
their eyes go big in their heads—
will it be me, the first,
or her? And when? How
long will you bear this hunger?
Sometimes
the eyes go wormy with waiting,
and at night they run away, but
we always find them in the hills
and drag them back to our fires.
At last
we have starved long enough.
We take the oldest first, a strong man
on each arm, each leg; we hold her face
over the fire, the head
jerking in smoke, her screaming
and twisting so weird, kids
mimic the squeals. Soon
she is food, enough
for our little clan: we cut her
carefully, keeping the best
for the hunters, strength
to defy the snows. Boys

get the next best pieces, then
the women and girls.
Old women come last: fingers
and toes, enough to hold them
till it's their turn. We
suck the broken bones
and burn them in our fires, Tierra
del Fuego; by the time the sun
betrays us to the dark,
everyone in the world
is happy.
The cucarachas come out
and taste the bloody earth,
twitching their whiskers. We chew
a few roaches, crunchy and tart,
and snuggle together, back to belly
for the long night, remembering
that somewhere in shadows
the Spirits watch: all-powerful, and
to be feared.

                3
This is how it's done: after the head-on,
drivers and passengers totaled;
after the flashing lights
bloody the neighborhood; after the sirens
yammer in, spewing stretchers;
after the tow truck jams carcasses
into the curb; after that,
it's her turn:
while vermin a hundred
million years old
swarm in the walls of air-
conditioned apartments,
she pulls up behind the Impala and begins.

First the whitewalls—hubcaps, wheels,
bolt by bolt, into the back
of her van: already
it's a good night's work,
and she's just begun.
Crowbar the trunk: the spare,
a suitcase, tool kit—gravy.
Then inside: blankets, jacket,
the C.B. A Cougar pulls over;
she bares her teeth: Listen,
this baby is mine,
you want business, take the Rabbit.
Now the front end: under
the sprung-open hood,
the socket wrenches:
alternator, battery, maybe
the carburetor . . . Well,
that's enough. The little guys
are getting pushy; leave them something,
hyenas, savages, they go
for scraps—tail lights,
wipers, spark plugs—all of that comes later,
then the dousing of gas,
and the campfire without marshmallows.

That is how it's done: now
it is night;
fires are burning carrion bones
and the tawny leather of Jaguars.
It is not dark
or quiet; but it is night,
and everywhere the immortal
cockroach is busy
surviving.

THE HAND-AX

Many things are at hand . . . wars, famines,
plagues, earthquakes . . . [but] let not your
mind be in any way disturbed; for these [are
but] signs of the end of the world . . .

—POPE GREGORY THE GREAT
to King Ethelbert of England, 601 A.D.

To those who fully admit the immortality of the
human soul, the destruction of our world will
not appear so dreadful.

—CHARLES DARWIN, *Autobiography, 1876*

Under the topsoil, shards,
brick, the rust
of civilizations: we're young enough
to wonder at those relics, the sharks,
the horseshoe crabs, but old enough to know
the fall of shamans, death
of temples—so
beyond the Book, beyond the Word,
beyond the Byzantines and Romans,
we dream of something older,
something walking upright, carrying
in the strong hand
this: one side round
for the palm, the cutting edge
fierce as a snarl, survivor
of a million years of sabertooth
and woolly mammoth, survivor of
those decadent flint arrowheads, bronze spears.
Hefting it now, here in the snow,
testing the ragged edge at Eighth Street
and Broadway, I know calluses, blood,

in the winter wind the smell
of red meat.
I pull on furs
and say goodbye to the fire in the cave,
to my woman and child,
to the old ones warming their skinny hands,
and step into bluster, scanning the smooth
snow till the tracks begin, doe and fawn,
bark fresh-nibbled. My moccasins
glide on the crust, the ax in my right hand
a constant urge; rabbits
skitter away, I sniff the air for tigers.
Two days' forest to the rising sun
my father's brother's clan
will join us for the bison kill
when the sun is making the long days;
but here there is only my own:
my spirits, my pines
green in the snow,
my animals.

They are upwind, chewing on saplings; I glide
across snow, nearly on them
before they turn—the quick alarm,
the scramble, awkward four-legged rush,
the doe gone like a spirit, but
the fawn is mine: the hand-ax
in one ecstatic blow
crushes the skull. I thong
her legs to a low limb,
slit the velvet throat, and drink,
warm to my moccasins.
Over my shoulders, the fawn's weight
breaks the crusted snow. Two days' forest
to the setting sun

Darwin's Ark

140

II. THE RUST OF CIVILIZATIONS

my brother's woman's clan will come
to my naked cave in the long nights
to paint the deer and bison on the walls,
blood-red and ochre, soot-black—we have
the art now, in our cunning fingers,
learned from my father's cousin's shamans,
five days' forest to the standing star, magic
so the beasts will not escape us ever:
we shall feed, and feed again, our spells
so powerful that the ax,
in the holy blessing of blood and fire,
will some day find a handle, a blade,
find caissons and wheels, and roll
across the land, working deadly
miracles.

Pulling at the zipper on my coat,
I slog through snow,
holding my ancient stone at Eighth Street
and Broadway. I know, if I drive the glaze
two hours to sunrise, I will find
the stones of Jericho and Babylon
and two hours to sunset
the brick of Bethlehem:
in all this wasted land
no lions now to lie down with the lambs.
The magic of the hand-ax stripped the forests,
plowed the grasslands, led us
to the mushroom skies, the boiling clouds—so now
the hardest of all revolutions:
spray-painting walls blood-red and ochre,
soot-black, defiance to the hunger of the ax,
knowing our hands must join
to put a force to No,
to Never:

after a million years of axes, we
are old enough to know
that when we die
we die forever,
and so, to join hands
to break the ax of Tribe, the power
of shamans to wreck our lives
and kill forever
with the radiation-death
of a hundred thousand years—
strong enough to say to all of them:
we are *Homo sapiens,* smart animal;
we will not flame to passion
in the firestorms of your frenzy.

IN ANDALUCÍA

"Very dry. Since three years,
little rain." Simple Spanish
so we'd understand. "The crops
are weak." His eyes tightened, the squint
of a grudging land.
We had come for the paintings, the animals
that fed Cro-Magnon here;
but for now, in the shade, we talked.
"A bad time," someone ventured,
needing to apologize for
the sparkling coast, our tall hotels.
"*Sí. Muy malo.*" A silence
as long as a sigh: the gray mountains
went on being mountains; in the distance
a truck was grinding its slow way up
and up—Andalucía, poorest province
of a poor country.
Sun shredded through
the cane shelter, the sweat of our climb
cooled, we thought of the long drive back,
twisting down to the coast;
we were ready for caves.
He gave us lanterns: splendid,
the gloomy halls, the chasms,
frozen cascades, the massive pillars
and icicles of stone, all
with their touristy names, Tower
of Pisa, Sword of Damocles, Bath
of the Moorish Queen. Then suddenly
all pretending stopped:
the limestone walls were human,
the hunter with his deadly bow
and his deathless prey, the graceful

running horse, the deer,
the long-horned mountain goat, the big fish
with little fish in its belly—
twenty thousand years
of eating. The cool
of the cave filtered
through our bones.
Emerging into glare,
we rubbed our arms like January,
making conversation:
"Do you guide in winter, too?"
"Yes. But very few
tourists in winter."
Muy poco, muy seco, muy malo, the stingy
history of this land: his eyes
did the painful squint again.
We started down.
The mountainsides were relentlessly
beautiful, corn and melons
fought the sun for life, peasants hoed
at the dusty earth: twenty
thousand years.

"BLACK-FOOTED FERRET ENDANGERED"

The taste in our mouths
is the feeding of tigers:
we're killing off eagles, too,
and whales.
How it all began: the way
our thumbs slowly came round
to grab for the throat, our toes
flattened for stalking, more than animal
cunning
swelling the skull—and then
the clever tools: the hand-ax,
the motor, more dangerous
than tigers.
It was only a matter of time
till the tools were a part of us
like glands, a million years of murder
creating this:
the pitiless face of the tiger
is our own face grinning
with gears.

THE FAITH-HEALER SPEAKS

The laying-on of hands: faith
that could move these barren hills
pulses through our fingertips,
and Darwin's demon apes of hell
howl the name of blasphemy.
We cast them out—yea, and the Serpent
who deceiveth the world, that
whoredom sitting on the waters,
with whom the kings of earth
have committed fornication, our faith
will cast it out! For so it was
by that little creek in Tennessee,
three hundred of the faithful come
marching to Zion in the August sun,
to pray above our crippled brother
seven raptured hours, and sing
    All hail the power of Jesus' name
till every hill in Tennessee
believed; and sisters in the throng, adrift
in all that heat and joy, were fainting for love
of the Lord, and men with muscles like the rocks
in God's good earth
watered the weeds with tears;
and when at last our hands came down
and touched those withered legs,
the afflicted brother stared around
with eyes that rolled with the love
of Jesus—and slowly rose, *rose*,
till he was on his knees,
our hymns still ringing off the hills:
    My faith looks up to Thee—
and then, in the heavenly current
coursing through our fingers, that

chosen man
set his teeth and rose again—
rose upright, in a tide of holy pain,
to stand on his own feet—stood there
a minute by the clock, before he slid
to grass! Praises, then, our praises rang
across the state of Tennessee—
for the Lord healeth those that are broken, He
telleth the number of the stars
and calleth them by their names—oh, Lord,
ravish our hearts with love
in the perfume of Thine ointments, in honey
and milk, in the savor
of saffron and pomegranates, come
to us now, Lord, come
as You did that sunny day in Tennessee—
come to us now as You came
to the halt and lame, to the woman
blind with cataracts, five hours in prayer, all
the faithful on that hilltop
shouting love to heaven, till
the demon shrieked aloud
and she was Saved, staring
into the sun till her dead eyes found
visions, omens crawling in the sky
that no one else in all that throng could see.

For so it has been, too,
here in the City of Angels, Zion of the West,
home of our Tabernacle, borne
from Tennessee, to fight
the poison plagues of Darwin on
the shores of this great ocean—here too
we have touched the fevered and palsied, here
we have said to the blind and bent:

"Thy faith hath made thee whole."
This boy, now,
fair and virginal, undefiled by woman, yet
possessed by the demon called
in the Godless clinic, "diabetes"—
this child was Saved,
as clear as Jesus' Word, washed
in the blood of the Lamb, as ready
for heaven as earth—the boy
had prayed with us, and his father
prayed, until their faith grew strong; and
here in these browning hills, we gathered
the faithful in our hundreds, chanting
till sunset:
      Praise God from Whom all blessings flow—
and the father, in that hour of triumph,
tears of good tidings on his cheeks,
called above the chanting,
"Come out of the boy, thou unclean spirit!"
And at that cry of victory,
he threw away the pills, those ugly
relics of his doubt—
and the boy cried out, rejoicing!

But oh, ye children of the light—
what terrors after sunset, in the hours
when Satan stalks the heathen dark
wherein the beasts of the forest move,
when Darwin's monkeys squeal their dirty lust,
and lions roaring after their prey do seek
the meat of God. The boy
had schooled with infidels, his faith
was thin like his youth, not robust
like his father's manly Grace—after two nights
the child would not breathe as he should,

his tongue went thick, perverse. Seven
of the faithful stayed always
and chanted at his bed till dawn, and he waxed
stronger for a moment here, a minute there—
then wavered, waned, refused to sing the hymns.
"Father," he whispered,
in a voice that spoke the spells of midnight,
"Father, give me the pills"—we heard the Serpent
slithering among us: the smell
of evil filled the room. Air! Light! We rushed
the boy in blankets to the hills
and faced him to the rising sun, and chanted,
  Nearer, my God, to Thee . . .
"Give me the pills," he whispered. But
his father's faith held strong; he cradled
the small head in his arms and sang,
  Holy, holy, holy, Lord God Almighty!
  Early in the morning our songs shall rise to Thee!

By the third verse, morning smog
had shut off the sun,
and in the swirling mist the demon rose,
Darwin's great beast rose before us,
scarlet with abominations—Satan
passed his hand over the boy's
sick faith: cold
settled in his limbs.

Oh, Lord,
Thou art Alpha and Omega, beginning and end,
and what is man, that Thou art mindful of him?

But yet he is not dead—the boy
only sleeps in the Lord. Tomorrow
he will rise again, our strength

will quicken his, the father's
sainthood will cast out this demon, Death,
and the boy will wake: here, on this
same hill, here in the sun in the City of Angels,
a thousand of the faithful sing from dawn
to sunset, praising the bountiful Lord,
and tomorrow we shall command this child to rise
and glorify God on earth, his body whole and strong,
his faith healed by the laying-on of hands,
the abiding prayer: tomorrow, yes,
tomorrow *he will rise.*

DARWIN'S BESTIARY

PROLOGUE

Animals tame and animals feral
prowled the Dark Ages in search of a moral:
the canine was Loyal, the lion was Virile,
rabbits were Potent and gryphons were Sterile.
Sloth, Envy, Gluttony, Pride—every peril
was fleshed into something phantasmic and rural,
while Courage, Devotion, Thrift—every bright laurel
crowned a creature in some mythological mural.

Scientists think there is something immoral
in singular brutes having meat that is plural:
beasts are mere beasts, just as flowers are floral.
Yet between the lines there's an implicit demurral;
the habit stays with us, albeit it's puerile:
when Darwin saw squirrels, he saw more than Squirrel.

1. THE ANT

The ant, Darwin reminded us,
defies all simple-mindedness:
Take nothing (says the ant) on faith,
and never trust a simple truth.
The PR men of bestiaries
eulogized for centuries
this busy little paragon,
nature's proletarian—
but look here, Darwin said: some ants
make slaves of smaller ants, and end
exploiting in their peonages
the sweating brows of their tiny drudges.

Thus the ant speaks out of both
sides of its mealy little mouth:
its example is extolled
to the workers of the world,
but its habits also preach
the virtues of the idle rich.

2. THE WORM

Eyeless in Gaza, earless in Britain,
lower than a rattlesnake's belly-button,
deaf as a judge and dumb as an audit:
nobody gave the worm much credit
till Darwin looked a little closer
at this spaghetti-torsoed loser.
Look, he said, a worm can feel
and taste and touch and learn and smell;
and ounce for ounce, they're tough as wrestlers,
and love can turn them into hustlers,
and as to work, their labors are mythic,
small devotees of the Protestant Ethic:
they'll go anywhere, to mountains or grassland,
south to the rain forests, north to Iceland,
fifty thousand to every acre
guzzling earth like a drunk on liquor,
churning the soil and making it fertile,
earning the thanks of every mortal:
proud *Homo sapiens,* with legs and arms—
his whole existence depends on worms.
So, History, no longer let
the worm's be an ignoble lot
unwept, unhonored, and unsung.
Moral: even a worm can turn.

3. THE RABBIT

a. Except in distress, the rabbit is silent,
    but social as teacups: no hare is an island.
        (Moral:
        silence is golden—or anyway harmless;
        rabbits may run, but never for Congress.)

b. When a rabbit gets miffed, he bounds in an orbit,
    kicking and scratching like—well, like a rabbit.
        (Moral:
        to thine own self be true—or as true as you can;
        a wolf in sheep's clothing fleeces his skin.)

c. He populates prairies and mountains and moors,
    but in Sweden the rabbit can't live out of doors.
        (Moral:
        to know your own strength, take a tug at your shackles;
        to understand purity, ponder your freckles.)

d. Survival developed these small furry tutors;
    the morals of rabbits outnumber their litters.
        (Conclusion:
        you needn't be brainy, benign, or bizarre
        to be thought a great prophet. Endure. Just endure.)

4. THE GOSSAMER

Sixty miles from land the gentle trades
that silk the Yankee clippers to Cathay
sift a million gossamers, like tides
of fluff above the menace of the sea.

These tiny spiders spin their bits of webbing
and ride the air as schooners ride the ocean;
the *Beagle* trapped a thousand in its rigging,
small aeronauts on some elusive mission.

The Megatherium, done to extinction
by its own bigness, makes a counterpoint
to gossamers, who breathe us this small lesson:
for survival, it's the little things that count.

EUPHORIAS

> *I heard a child, a little under four years old, when*
> *asked what was meant by being in good spirits,*
> *answer, "It is laughing, talking, and kissing."*
> —CHARLES DARWIN, *The Expression*
> *of the Emotions in Man and Animals*

1. WALDORF-ASTORIA EUPHORIA, THE JOY OF BIG CITIES

> *Joy, when intense, leads to various purposeless*
> *movements—to dancing about, clapping the*
> *hands, stamping, etc.*   —IBID.

You feel so good, you stop walking:
they swirl around you, racing the 6:15.
You bless them all with a smile
you cannot explain: they are suddenly
precious. You look around, with your alien eyes,
at forty floors of windows where
they are laughing, talking, and kissing: you realize
they are priceless. You feel them
under the pavement, riding the uptown express,
straphanging bodies waving
like kelp, and you know
they are irreplaceable; you think of them
all over town, bursting
with unused happiness, and you clap,
and clap again, and clapping, you sing
a song you thought you'd forgotten, and your waist

moves gently, like jonquils, and your hand
catches her fingertips, and she smiles, her arms
moving like willows,
and the fruitseller dances with apples,
crying a musical language, and a girl
with a bongo comes on with rhythm,
her hips moving like wheatfields, and
the hardhats come up from the manholes,
their bodies moving like jackhammers,
and Chinese voices like windchimes
sing to the women from San Juan
who gather around like palm trees, and the cops
have cordoned the street and are dancing
with women from Minnesota,
their thighs as seductive as seaweed;
and you know that sooner or later
this had to happen: that somehow
it would all break out, all that pent-up
joy, and people would sing and hold hands,
their bodies swerving like taxis,
and the music inside their heads
would fill the streets with dancing,
clapping hands, and stamping;
and you sing another chorus
of we,
hey, we,
yes, we,
I said we
are all
we've got.

2. HUNKYDORIA EUPHORIA, THE JOY OF HAVING IT MADE

*From the excitement of pleasure, the circulation
becomes more rapid, the eyes are bright, and
the colour of the face rises.* —IBID.

You're sweating it out: the last time
it was never received;
it was lost in the files; sent
to the wrong department.
If you get there by noon, surely
it will be all right; but the seconds
are deadly. At ten to twelve
You reach the office, and of course
there's a line.
You inch along; at noon you touch
mahogany, and just as you feared, there is
some difficulty, a shuffling
of papers: you feel
the invisible stars
swing through their long
cold journey. Finally—
you can hardly believe it—
it's there! the very thing! the thing itself!
and the holy rubber stamp
falls like a benediction,
and you hear, above the ceiling,
the seraphim rejoicing,
and you smooth your hair
and borrow a debonair manner
and step through the frosted door
so deliberately,
no one would ever guess
that right there under your shirt
the sun is dancing on water.

HOW EVOLUTION CAME TO INDIANA

In Indianapolis they drive
five hundred miles and end up
where they started: survival
of the fittest. In the swamps
of Auburn and Elkhart,
in the jungles of South Bend,
one-cylinder chain-driven runabouts fall
to air-cooled V-4's, 2-speed gearboxes,
16-horse flat-twin midships engines—
carcasses left behind
by monobloc motors, electric starters,
3-speed gears, six cylinders, 2-chain drive,
overhead cams, supercharged
to 88 miles an hour in second gear, the age
of Leviathan . . .
> *There is grandeur in this view of life,*
> *as endless forms*
> *most beautiful and wonderful*
> *are being evolved.*
And then
the drying up, the panic,
the monsters dying: Elcar, Cord,
Auburn, Duesenberg, Stutz—somewhere
out there, the chassis of Studebakers,
Marmons, Lafayettes, Bendixes, all
rusting in high-octane smog,
ashes to ashes, they
end up where they started.

MR. EXTINCTION, MEET MS. SURVIVAL

They're always whispering:
missing buttons, crow's-feet,
rust—
and I try to ignore them at first,
but they keep it up:
half-soles, dry rot,
biopsies, Studebakers—
that does it,
and I have to yell back:
virgin wool! fresh coffee! tennis balls!
new pennies! robins!
and that holds them awhile,
but they always come again,
sometimes at night, sometimes
in crowded elevators: *loose shingles,*
they whine, *soil erosion, migraines,*
dented fenders. I hold my ears
and shout: *high tide! fresh bread!*
new shoes! oranges! and people around me nod
and straighten their shoulders and smile,
and I think for a moment I've won—
but of course you never win,
and it gets to be almost a game:
they give me *oil spills,*
sewage sludge, tobacco smoke;
I come back with *swimming pools,*
butterflies, cornfields!
They give me *Calcutta,*
Gary, Coney Island;
I rattle off *Windermere,*
Isfahan, Bloomington! But
by the time I'm at work

it gets serious, all
lapsed memberships and *auto graveyards*
and *partial dentures* and *sub-
committees* and *leaves in the eaves,*
and right there at my desk I bellow:
daffodils! and *sailboats!* and *Burgundy!*
and *limestone!* and *birch trees!* and *robins,
damn it, robins!* and my boss
pats me on the shoulder, and my secretary
takes it in shorthand, and everywhere
efficiency doubles, I'm doing it, after all,
for them. And yet,
deep down, I know, in fact,
it's no more daffodils than it's half-soles—
what it really is,
is morning without a hangover
but an even chance of rain,
it's a cost-of-living raise
and a slight case of heartburn. Well,
we all know about
the slow leak, the scratch
on our favorite record,
the 7:12 forty minutes late, sure—
but passenger pigeons? Studebakers? That's
going too far,
we have our pride, our good
intentions, our metabolism, we won't
be shunted off with clipper ships
and whooping cranes, we're going
to hang in there, all of us, because
the robins may be showing wear,
but still, by god,
they are robins.

HOW MY LIGHT IS SPENT

Eyes are certainly not necessary to animals
having subterranean habits.

—CHARLES DARWIN, *The Origin of Species*

On the subway you thought
it couldn't happen to you. But now
the doctors are dazzling in white, Science
burns in your eyeball: white-equals-black.
At last
the true dark falls like an eyelid.
In the waiting room, your hand reaches out
for a white cane: the dark
is an old home, you live there
in the caves of childhood,
with your lovers in lamplight,
with the brown hair of your beautiful sisters.
In the down elevator you think:
but everybody sees. What you see
in the shine of the car is Science,
dazzling in white, Darwin
dissecting his blind
barnacles; you see moles, bats,
fins in the murk
of a thousand fathoms; now
you know better. At the door
daylight staggers you; hands over face,
you find the subway. There,
in dim fluorescence: the Byzantine
mosaic of the walls,
I-beams rich with perfect rivets,
the silver splendor of the rails,
and from a green bench, as the gorgeous
graffiti scream in,
a woman in a crimson sweater
rising like the sun.

"SEA OTTER SURVIVAL ASSURED"

We saw several sea otters, the fur of which is
held in such high estimation.
　　　—CHARLES DARWIN, *The Voyage of the* Beagle

The Fish and Game Department reports 591 otters
in the current census, 94 higher than last year.
　　　—NEWS REPORT

A million years before Darwin
this weasel slid into the sea
to tear at the brooding oysters
and roll wet eyes for the gliding
shadows of dim sea-monsters.
For a million years of birth
in the brine of the north Pacific
the fair exchange was fur
like ermine. When the big boats came,
bearing the hairless hunters,
the fittest betrayed his survival:
his skin was worth more than his life.

In a fog, five hundred otters
are nudging their young along
the coastline of California,
while monstrous in bed, the Pacific
is breaking with billions of faces,
turbaned men from the Punjab,
brown-eyed girls with rice bowls,
horsemen waving their rifles—

and five hundred otters thrashing
the bell of a bedside alarm.

Survival assured: across
the pacific waves of blanket
someone as blond as hope
speaks from the edges of sleeping:
"Morning is out there again,
on the other side of the curtains."

Natural Selection,
we have come through another night,
come to one more day.

ON THE *BEAGLE*

Some people hold the world
in their fingertips, and
are part of what they hold.

The *Beagle* set sail
to easy summer—five years on sea
and land the watchful man
from Cambridge put
his fingers on a universe
of cuttlefish, sea-slugs, condors,
the ancient monsters' bones,
Megatherium, Mastodon: all
fixed forever in immutable forms, creatures
of a benign Intelligence.
It was written.

But the young man put his fingers on
the pulse of rivers, coral reefs,
pampas and mountains,
the flotsam of earthquakes—and
on futures of learning, from
pigeons' plumage, the beaks of finches, bones
of rabbits and ducks—decades
of learning,
dissecting ten thousand
barnacles—pondering:
"If we choose to let
conjecture run wild, then animals—
our fellow brethren in pain,
disease, death, suffering, and famine—
they may partake from our origin

in one common ancestor:
we may be all
netted together.'"

The *Beagle* labored on: in the winter
of Cape Horn,
twenty-three days of beating
against the icy bluster
came to broken boats
and spoiled collections.
The good ship rode to shelter—
and there on a rocky point
of Tierra del Fuego, naked
in snow, a mother
suckled her child
("whilst the sleet fell and thawed
on her naked bosom, and on the skin
of her naked baby")—there, in a little band,
stood
"man in his primitive wildness,"
ringed by the dark beech forest:
"As they threw their arms wildly
around their heads,
their long hair streaming,
they seemed the troubled spirits
of another world."
There
in the Bay of Good Success,
Charles Darwin, on the foredeck of the *Beagle*,
our future in his freezing fingertips,
stared into the faces
of our past.

THE VOYAGE HOME

The social instincts . . .
naturally lead to the golden rule.
                    —CHARLES DARWIN, *The Descent of Man*

1

Holding her steady, into the pitch and roll,
in raw Midwestern hands ten thousand tons
of winter wheat for the fall of Rome,
still swallowing the hunger of the war:
the binnacle glows like an open fire,
east-southeast and steady,
Anderssen, the Viking mate,
belaboring me for contraband,
my little book of Einstein, that
"Commie Jew." (So much for the social instincts,
pacifism, humanism, the frail
and noble causes.) I speak my piece
for western civ: light bends . . .
stars warp . . . mass converts . . .
"Pipe dreams," says the Dane, "pipe dreams."
"Well, mate, remember,
those Jewish dreams made nightmares
out of Hiroshima, and
blew us out of uniform, alive."
He stomps down off the bridge; some day
he'll fire me off his rusty
liberty: I read too much.
The ocean tugs and wrestles with
ten thousand deadweight tons
of charity, trembling on
degrees and minutes. Anderssen
steams back in with coffee, to
contest the stars with Einstein, full ahead.
We haven't come to Darwin.

2

Freezing on the flying bridge,
staring at the night for nothing,
running lights of freighters lost
in a blur of blowing snow,
we hold on through the midnight watch,
waiting out the bells.
With Einstein in our wake, the tricks
are easier: liberty
churns on, ten knots an hour,
toward Rome. One starry night
we ride at last with Darwin on
the *Beagle:* endless ocean, sea
sickness, revelations
of Toxodon and Megalonyx—a voyage
old as the Eocene, the watery death
of Genesis. The going
gets rough again, the threat of all those bones
churning the heavy swells: Anderssen,
a true believer, skeptical,
and Darwin trapped in a savage earthquake,
the heave of coastal strata conjuring
the wreck of England, lofty houses gone,
government in chaos,
violence and pillage through the land,
and afterward,
fossils gleaming white along
the raw ridges.
"Limeys." Anderssen puts his benediction
to empire: "Stupid Limeys." After that
we breathe a bit and watch the stars and tell
sad stories of the death of tribes, the bones,
the countless bones: we talk about
the war, we talk about
extinction.

3

Okinawa, Iwo Jima:
slouching toward Tokyo, the only good Jap
is a dead Jap.
We must get the bomb, Einstein writes
to F.D.R., waking from
the dreams of peace, the noble causes:
get it first, before
the Nazis do. (The only good Nazi
is an extinct Nazi.)
At the death of Hiroshima, all day long
we celebrate extinction, chugalugging
free beer down at the PX, teen-
age kids in khaki puking pints
of three-point-two in honor
of the fire: no more island-hopping now
to the murderous heart of empire.
Later, in the luxury of peace,
the bad dreams come. "Certainly,"
Darwin broods, "no fact
in the long history of the world
is so startling as the wide and repeated
extermination
of its inhabitants."

4

Off somewhere to starboard, the Canaries,
Palma, Tenerife: sunrise
backlights the rugged peaks, as Darwin,
twenty-two years old, gazes at
the clouds along the foothills.
Longitudes ease westward; it's
my birthday: twenty-two years old
as Tenerife falls into the sunset,
I'm as greedy for the old world

as Darwin for the new, Bahia, Desire,
the palms and crimson flowers
of the Mediterranean, clear water
dancing with mines. Ahead of us
a tanker burns; the war
will never end.

                5
"You talk a lot," says the melancholy Dane.
"You sure you're not Jewish yourself?
You got a funny name."
"Well, mate, I'm pure Celtic on one side,
pure Orphan on the other: therefore half
of anything at all—Jewish, Danish,
what you will: a problem, isn't it,
for Hitler, say, or the Klan,
or even Gregor Mendel, sweating out the summer
in his pea patch?"
The fact is, I know those ancestors
floating through my sleep:
an animal that breathed water,
had a great swimming tail,
an imperfect skull, undoubtedly
hermaphrodite . . . I slide
through all the oceans with these kin,
salt water pulsing in my veins,
and aeons follow me into the trees:
a hairy, tailed quadruped,
arboreal in its habits, scales
slipping off my flanks, the angle of my spine
thrust upward, brain
bulging the skull until
I ride the *Beagle*
down the eastern trades to earthquake,
to naked cannibals munching red meat

and Spanish grandees with seven names
crushing the fingers of slaves.
Who are my fathers? mothers? who
will I ever father?
I will sire the one in my rubber sea-boots, who
has sailed the seas and come
to the bones of Megatherium.
From the war of nature, from famine and death,
we stand at last creators
of ourselves: "The greatest
human satisfaction," Darwin muses, "is derived
from following the social instincts." Well,
the thing I want to father
is the rarest, most difficult thing
in any nature: I want to be,
knee-deep in these rivers of innocent blood,
a decent animal.

6

Landfall: Yankee liberty discharges
calories on the docks, where kids
with fingers formed by hairy
quadrupeds cross
mumbo jumbo on their chests
and rub small signs for hope
and charity.
Liberty, sucked empty of its
social instincts, follows the *Beagle*
down the empty avenues of water
to amber waves of grain, to feed
the children of our fathers' wars,
new generations of orphans, lives
our quaint old-fashioned bombs
had not quite ended.

7

Alone
on the fantail
I hear the grind of rigging, and
Darwin is beside me, leaning on the rail,
watching the wake go phosphorescent.
We've been out five years, have seen
the coral islands, the dark skins
of Tahiti; I have questions.
"Darwin," I whisper, "tell me now,
have you entered into the springs of the sea,
or have you walked in search of the depth?
Did you give the gorgeous wings to peacocks,
or feathers to the ostrich?
Have you given the horse his strength
and clothed his neck with thunder?
Who has put wisdom in the inward parts,
and given understanding to the heart?
Answer me."
The breeze is making eddies in the mist,
and out of those small whirlwinds come the words:
"I have walked along the bottom of the sea
wrenched into the clouds at Valparaiso;
I have seen the birth of islands and
the build of continents; I
know the rise and fall of mountain ranges,
I understand the wings of pigeons,
peacock feathers, finches; my mind creates
general laws out of large
collections of facts."
The rigging sighs a little: God
is slipping away without
saying goodbye, goodbye to Jewish dreams.
"But the activities of the mind,"

Darwin murmurs, "are one of the bases of conscience."
Astern the pious Spaniards go on praying
and crushing the fingers of slaves; somewhere
the Mylodon wanders away,
out of the animal kingdom and
into the empire of death.
For five billion years
we have seen the past, and
it works.

8

So this is the final convoy
of the social instincts: the next
time missiles fly to Rome,
they will carry Einstein's dream of fire,
and afterward there will be no need
for liberties, hope, or charity.
Now we ride the oceans of
imagination, all horizon
and no port. Darwin
will soon be home, his five-year
voyage on this little brig
all over; but when will I
be home, when will I arrive
at that special creation: a decent animal?
The land is failing the horizons, and
we only know to take the wheel
and test the ancient strength of human struggle,
remembering that we ourselves, the wonder
and glory of the universe, bear
in our lordly bones the indelible stamp
of our lowly
origin.

Let There Be Light

I. THE BIBLE RETOLD FOR GROWNUPS

GATHERING AT THE RIVER

Is it
crossing over Jordan
to a city of light, archangels
ceaselessly trumpeting over
the heavenly choirs: perpetual Vivaldi,
jasper and endless topaz and amethyst,
the Sistine ceiling seven days a week,
the everlasting smirk
of perfection?

Is it
the river Styx,
darkness made visible, fire
that never stops: endless murder
too merciless to kill,
massacres on an endless loop,
the same old victims always
coming back for more?

Or is it the silky muck
of Wabash and Maumee, the skirr
and skim of blackbirds,
fields of Queen Anne's lace
and bumblebees? Well,
go out once more, and feel
the crumble of dry loam,
fingers and soil slowly becoming
the same truth: there in the hand
is our kinship with oak, our bloodline
to cattle. Imagine,

not eons of boredom or pain,
but honest earth-to-earth;
and when our bodies rise again,
they will be wildflowers, then rabbits,
then wolves, singing a perfect love
to the beautiful, meaningless moon.

EVE

Clever, he was, so slick
he could weave words into sunshine.
When he murmured another refrain
of that shimmering promise, "You
shall be as gods," something with wings
whispered back in my heart,
and I crunched the apple—a taste so good
I just had to share it with Adam,
and all of a sudden
we were naked.
Oh, yes, we were nude before, but now,
grabbing for fig leaves, we knew
that we knew too much, just as the slippery
serpent said—so we crouched all day
under the rhododendrons, trembling
at something bleak and windswept in our bellies
that soon we'd learn to call by its right name:
fear.
God was furious with the snake
and hacked off his legs, on the spot.
And for us
it was thorns and thistles,
sweat of the brow, dust
to dust returning. In that sizzling
skyful of spite whirled
the whole black storm of the future:
the flint knife in Abel's heart,
the incest that swelled us into a tribe,
a nation, and
brought us all, like driven lambs,
straight to His flood.
I blamed it on human nature, even then,
when there were only two humans around,

and if human nature was a mistake,
whose mistake was it? *I* didn't ask
to be cursed with curiosity, I only wanted
the apple,
and of course that promise—to be
like gods. But then,
maybe we are like gods.
Maybe we're all exactly like gods.
And maybe that's our really original
sin.

AN EYE FOR AN EYE

"Are you saved?" he asks me,
sunrise in the corner of his eye,
a snag at the edge of his voice.
In a blur of memory, I see the others:
the preacher who used to trounce my tender sins,
kids at church camp, their brimstone choirs
shrill with teenage lust gone underground,
true believers come knocking to tell me
that flaming hell is real.
And those twisted faces on the tube:
Christian gunmen in Beirut, their hot eyes
exploding in the beds of sleeping children;
the righteous hatreds of Belfast, lighting
Irish eyes like a tenement fire;
the eyes of the Ayatollah, squinting with joy
at the blood of his blindfolded prisoners.
It smolders in the windows of the soul,
that holy blaze, never so bright
as in human sacrifice,
never so proud as in crimson crusades,
the glorious, godlike destruction.

NOAH

Seed of Methuselah,
already six hundred years old,
more than a little weary
from all that virtuous living—then
a finger out of the clouds pokes down at him,
and a Voice full of blood and bones
bullies the stony hillsides:
"Make thee an ark of gopher wood . . ."
Details follow, in that same
bossy baritone: "The boat shall be
four hundred fifty feet long
seventy-five feet wide
three decks
one window
one door."

And then
the Voice tells him why.

His sons, Shem, Ham, and Japheth, just
cannot handle this news.
"He's going to drown them all?" Japheth whispers,
"Every last woman and child? What for?"
Noah's mind is not what it used to be; lately
it strays like a lost lamb, his ancient voice
a bleat: "Ahh—
wickedness, I think that's
what He said—yes, wickedness."
Too vague for Japheth: "But wicked how? I mean,
what are the charges?"
The old brow wrinkles again. "Evil, that's
what He said. Corruption. Violence."
"Violence! What do you call

this killer flood? He's going to murder
the lot of them, just
for making a few mistakes? For being—human?"
Now Japheth is really riled. Being the youngest,
he still has a lot of drinking pals around—
Enos and Jared, and sexy Adah
and his pretty young neighbor,
Zillah—together they'd put away
many a goatskin of red wine
under the big desert stars. Besides,
being a kid, a mere ninety years old,
he still likes to stump his father
with embarrassing questions. "Listen,
Dad, I thought you said He
was omniscient—well, then,
wouldn't He have foreseen all this? And if He did,
why did He make us the way we are
in the first place?"

"Ours not to reason why," says Shem, the firstborn
and something of a prig. "Ours but to build the ark."
"That's another thing," Japheth scowls. "Just
what *is* an ark? I mean,
we're desert people, after all—nomads,
living out here in this miserable dry scrub
with our smelly goats and camels—
I never saw a boat in my life."
"I saw one once," Noah quavers,
"but I don't remember it very well,
that was four hundred years ago—
or was it five, let's see . . ."
"It can't be that hard," says Ham,
always the practical one. "An ordinary boat,
we'll mock one up. You need a keel, that's it,
you begin with a keel of gopher wood,

and the rest is easy—ribs, then planks,
pitch, decking. Don't worry, Dad,
I'll handle it."

So finally they have themselves an ark,
and God says, "Good work, Noah, now
get the animals—clean beasts, seven of a kind,
unclean, just two, but make sure
they're male and female, you got that straight?
And hurry it up, so I can get
the drowning started."
Noah was hoping the animals
would be easy, but Japheth
knows better. "Dad,
did He say *every* animal?"
"Every animal," Noah repeats,
quoting Authority. "Every living thing
of all flesh—fowl,
cattle, creeping things. Plus
food enough for a year."

Think of it—they're living out there
in that gritty wilderness, and all of a sudden
they're supposed to come up with two elephants.
Or is it more?
"Shem," Japheth calls. "Is the elephant
a clean or an unclean animal?
If it's clean, that means seven of them
and the ark is in trouble. And how
about rhinos? And hippos? What do we do
about the dinosaurs? How do we get a brontosaurus
up the gangplank?" Japheth
loves raising problems that Noah
hasn't thought of at all. "Pandas—kids
love pandas, we can't let them die out,

but how do we get two of them here
in a hurry, all the way from China?
And, oh, by the way, Dad,
how are we going to keep the lions
away from the lambs?"

It's not just a headache; it's a nightmare.
Just think of poor Ham, after all of his angst
and sweat getting the ark assembled, and then
having to trudge off to the Congo and the Amazon
to round up all those tricky
long-tailed leapers, there in the jungle greenery—
gibbons, orangutans, gorillas, baboons, chimps,
howler monkeys, spider monkeys, squirrel monkeys,
capuchins, mandrills, tamarins . . .

And Shem, dutiful Shem, in charge
of the other mammals—the giraffes,
the horses, zebras, quaggas, tapirs, bison,
the pumas, bears, shrews, raccoons, weasels,
skunks, mink, badgers, otters, hyenas,
the rats, bats, rabbits, chipmunks, beavers—
thousands of species of mammals . . .

And Japheth out there on the cliffs and treetops
trying to snare the birds—the eagles,
condors, hawks, buzzards, vultures, and every
winged beauty in the rain forests—and bring them back,
chattering, twittering, fluttering around
on the top deck, thousands upon thousands
of hyperkinetic birds . . .

Two by two
they come strolling through:
antelope, buffalo, camel, dog,

egret, ferret, gopher, frog,
quail and wombat, sheep and goose,
turtle, nuthatch, ostrich, moose,
ibex, jackal, kiwi, lark,
two by two they board the ark.

Well, it's pretty clear, isn't it,
that there's a space problem here: a boat
only four hundred fifty feet long, already
buzzing and bleating and squeaking and mooing
and grunting and mewing and hissing and cooing
and croaking and roaring and peeping and howling
and chirping and snarling and clucking and growling—
and the crocodiles aren't back from the Nile
yet, or the iguanas from the islands,
or the kangaroos or koalas, or
the pythons or boas or cotton-mouth moccasins
or the thirty different species of rattlesnake
or the tortoises, salamanders, centipedes, toads . . .

It takes some doing, all that,
but Ham comes back with them.
And wouldn't you know,
it's Japheth who opens up, so to speak,
the can of worms. "Dad, there are thousands
of species of worms! Who's
going digging for them? And oh, yes,
how about the insects?"
"Insects!" Shem rebels at last,
"Dad, do we have to save *insects*?" Noah,
faithful servant, quotes the Word:
"Every living thing."
"But Dad, the cockroaches?"
Noah has all the best instincts
of a minor bureaucrat—he

is only following orders—the roaches
go aboard.

Japheth ticks away at his roster. "So far
we've got dragonflies, damselflies, locusts, and aphids,
grasshoppers, mantises, crickets, and termites . . .
Wait a minute—termites?
We're going to save termites, in a wooden boat?"
But Japheth knows that arguing with Noah
is like driving a nail into chicken soup. He shrugs
and carries on. "We've got lice,
beetles—God knows how many beetles.
We've got bedbugs, cooties, gnats, and midges,
horseflies, sawflies, bottleflies, fireflies.
We've got ants, bees, wasps, hornets—
can you imagine what it's going to be like
cooped up with *them* for a whole year?
But Dad, we haven't even scratched the surface.
There must be a million species
of insects out there.
Even if we unload all the other animals,
the insects alone will sink the ark!"

Ah, but the ark was not floating on fact,
it was floating on faith—that is to say,
on fiction. And in fiction, the insects
went aboard—*and* a year's supply
of hay for the elephants, a year's bananas
for the monkeys, and so on.
"Well, that's that," Japheth says,
"but you still haven't answered my question—
what will the meat-eaters eat?"
"We'll cross that bridge when we come to it,"
Noah replies, in history's
least appropriate trope,

"All aboard, now, it's starting
to sprinkle."

So the fountains of the great deep
were broken up, and the windows of heaven opened,
and the rain was upon the earth
forty days and forty nights,
and the ark was lifted up
and went upon the face of the waters—
and the drowning began.
Noah pretended not to know,
and so did Shem and Ham, so
it was only Japheth who keened
for Enos and Jared, still out there
somewhere, and for Adah and beautiful Zillah.
He was the first to peek
out of the one small window, and yes,
there it was, just the way fear
had been painting it on his eyelids ever since
that divine command: people fighting
for high ground, crazed beasts goring
and gnashing, serpents dangling from trees.
Finally, Shem, Ham, and Noah
and the four nameless wives
couldn't resist—they looked out the window, too,
and watched their friends
hugging in love and panic until
they all went under. Japheth caught
one final glimpse, and of course it had to be Zillah,
holding her baby over her head
till the water rolled over her
and she sank, and the baby
splashed a little, and then
there was silence upon the waters,
and God was well pleased.

They all turned away from the window, Noah
and his sons and the weeping women,
and no one would look into anyone's eyes
for many days.

Twelve hard months that strange menagerie lived
in the ark, the sixteen thousand hungry birds
lusting for the two million insects,
and the twelve thousand snakes and lizards
nipping at the seven thousand mammals,
and everyone slipping and sliding around
on the sixty-four thousand worms
and the one hundred thousand spiders—
and Noah driving everyone buggy, repeating
every morning, as if he'd just thought of it,
"Well, we're all in the same boat."
It was a long, long year
for those weary men and their bedraggled wives,
feeding the gerbils and hamsters, cleaning
the thousands of cages, keeping the jaguars
away from the gazelles, the grizzlies away
from the cottontails—everything aboard, after all,
was an endangered species.
But finally the waters subsided,
the dove fluttered off and never returned,
the gangplank slid down to Ararat,
and the animals scrambled out to the muddy,
corpse-ridden earth.

And Noah, burning a lamb on his altar
under that mocking rainbow, cannot forget
that he rescued the snakes and spiders, but
he let Enoch and Jubal
and Cainan and Lamech and
their wives and innocent children

go to a soggy grave.
And Noah knows, in his tired bones,
that now he will have to be fruitful once more,
and multiply, and replenish the earth
with a pure new race of people who
would never, *never* sin again,
for if they did,
all that killing would be for nothing,
a terrible embarrassment
to God.

HEAVENLY BODY
Halley's Comet, 1985, 1986

1

"Comet," from the Greek, means
a curve
of golden hair.
Plotting the curves:
parabolas of calf,
ellipses of thigh, and
little worlds adrift
in mystery—
what is the secret name
for the bend inside the knee,
and what is the word
for the arc between
the first and second toe?
Springtime:
out there on the sand
horseshoe crabs are clattering
their armor-plated love—
everything that matters
will return.

2

In our dark ages, comets burn
their warnings in the sky,
famines, plagues, the death of kings—
or nothing in our lives
except our lives.
Massaging her back: a love song
played along a xylophone of spine,
feeling out the valleys of her nape,
the graceful curve of shoulder—but
what do we call

that little tuck behind the shoulder blades,
and what is the word for the tempting
dimples in her loins?
      Autumn:
      a million monarchs
      fly their royal destiny
      across the continent, returning
      again, and yet again
      for love.

      3
      "Perihelion" is also Greek, meaning
      the closest we can get, our inner
      outer limit, the strongest pull of all
      our gravity.
Deep inside her, everything
is silk and velvet, spring
and fall, rhythms in
the memory of hips—but
what is the word
for that sudden tightness in the throat,
and what do we call
the craving in the heart
just before the murky sky
showers a thousand stars across our bed?
      Spring: mayflies brood upon
      the tragedy of evening and
      the grand design of their
      return.
      Fall: the golden-haired traveler reappears,
      shining toward perihelion,
      and vermilion floats
      from the fingers of maple trees
      to mulch again our secret words
      for love.

SARAH

You remember me,
the tough-luck wife of Abraham—
a beauty, they called me
in the old days in Egypt, a flower
fit for Pharaohs. But now
I'm just a gray granny who pesters you
with the tales they used to tell
around the evening fire . . .

The story goes
that after the great flood drained away—
drained away to *where*, I always wondered—
then Noah came limping down the gangplank,
feeling older than old, downright ante-
diluvian, and looked around, left and right.
Everywhere he looked
he saw nothing with those cloudy eyes
but landscapes of corpses and skeletons.
So who could blame him if he drank too much
and sprawled around in the buff all day? I mean,
given that heavy load of guilt,
friends and neighbors gone to mushy death,
wouldn't you?
Anyway, that's all the poor guy did
for over three hundred years until,
just twenty candles shy of Methuselah's record,
he finally turned up his toes.
Meanwhile, Shem, Ham, and Japheth
and their anonymous wives were going at it
day and night, getting the begetting going
again, the way the Lord commanded. Sure enough,
Shem—a hundred years old after the flood—
Shem begat a son he named

Arphaxad.
In due time
Arphaxad begat Salah
who begat Eber
who begat Peleg—
and so it went, for another hundred years,
until Terah begat my husband, Abram,
and Abram's brother, the father of Lot.

When he came to itchy manhood, Abram
looked upon me with favor—I
was an eyeful in those days, remember—and
he made me his wife.
We all moved off to Canaan,
Abram in the country to the west, Lot near a more
sophisticated town called Sodom.
And we prospered.
But then
God changed Abram's name to Abraham,
and told him, "Look, I've heard
that Sodom over there is a swamp of perversion,
Gomorrah, too. If that's really true . . ."

We both knew God well enough to see
where this was heading.
We still remembered the flood, not
that long ago, after all.
We knew that when God
gets into a rage, He smites
everything in sight, rain falling
on the just and the unjust. Then
Abraham thought of his nephew Lot,
doing so well with his flocks and herds
over by Sodom,
so before God gets ten steps away,

he runs after Him, shouting,
"Lord! Lord! Wait a minute! How about
all the good folks over there? Family men,
chaste women, keepers of the Sabbath,
salt of the earth—
are you going to blast them right along
with the perverts? Listen,
there might be, say, fifty saints
in that poor town.
Wouldn't you save it, for their sakes?"
Oh, that was nervy enough, but then
I thought I'd collapse
when Abraham turns the screw again:
"Shall not . . ." he begins—I can see his legs
quivering as he says it—"Shall not
the judge of all the earth
do right?"

When I dare to look,
they're still nose to nose,
my poor Abe quaking like a weed in a windstorm,
but firm in his nephew's cause,
and God, gone white as a thunderhead, but so far
not losing His temper the way He always did
down in Egypt, blazing away
at everything that moved.
Pretty soon He nods a bit,
like a camel trader who's just been outwitted,
and mutters, "All right, Abraham,
you find me fifty diamonds
in that dirt, and I'll back off."
He turns to go, and finally
I can breathe again. But then
Abraham calls out,

"God! Yahweh! Listen! I'm a nothing,
I'm the dirt under your sandals,
I'm the ashes from your campfire,
I'm a pest, forgive me for asking,
I shouldn't mention it—but suppose,
just suppose I come up short by five, just five short,
what then, would you burn the place for five?"
God is a little quicker this time—
you know how it is, once you have
a deal cooking, things go easier—
and He says, gritting His teeth a little,
"All right, Abraham, Patriarch,
Father of My Nation, for forty-five
I'll save the slimy place."
But before I can relax,
Abe blurts out, not even pretending
to grovel, "How about forty?"
God comes right back,
"OK, forty,
forty's OK,"
and turns on His heel.

So this time when Abraham calls again, I figure
it's all up with us, he's gone too far,
you can't haggle like this, not
with the Lord Himself, not even
in the Middle East. But Abraham
goes all oily: "God, please, don't get mad,
but say now—how about thirty?"
God doesn't even turn around. "Thirty. Done."
And Abe: "Twenty? Twenty righteous souls,
twenty virtuous, circumcised, ram-killing,
bullock-burning, tithe-paying citizens
who love the Lord?"
God is slouching down our front path,

kicking stones. I can barely hear
His gruff voice: "All right. Agreed.
It's a deal."

And I pray to myself—quit
while you're still ahead, Abraham! This
is the Lord of flood and plague,
the jealous God, God of the flaming sword,
the God of pestilence, the Angel of Death,
you're playing with fire, enough, *enough!*

But he has to do it one more time,
old goat-seller, bargain-hunter,
carpet-buyer, his whole life an endless
flea market, it must have come over him
like a nervous tic, irresistible, his voice
full of the fever of wheeling and dealing, and of course
the unbearable fear of losing it all—
after so many years I recognize
the symptoms. "*God!*" he shouts.
My stomach cramps up, my eyes squeeze shut,
waiting for the end. "God,
don't get mad, I swear
this is the last time,
but wait—*how about ten?*"
And I catch the quick crackle of lightning,
the stench of burning flesh . . .
But no, it's only God's voice,
fading in the distance: "I will not
destroy it for ten's sake."

So that, at last, is that. Abraham
is still standing there in our gravel path,
sweat staining his summer robes.
I run to him and hug him, glad

for the little cakes I baked for God that morning,
glad for the fatted calf we killed
and fed Him, knowing that full bellies
make good tempers. But Abe is all unstrung
by the terrible chance he's taken.
As I lead him back to the tent like a cripple,
he mumbles again and again, how hard it is
to make the judge of all the earth
do right.

You can guess what happened next.
There hadn't even been a handshake,
let alone a contract, and like they say
out here in the Holy Land, a verbal deal
isn't worth the parchment it's written on.
So to make a long story short,
when Lot heard that God was reneging,
he got out of Sodom fast,
taking his wife and daughters
up to the mountains, an angel warning them
not to look back on that holy
holocaust. But when the red-hot coals
winged over Sodom, and the fire
began falling from heaven, Lot's wife
just *had* to check it out, just for a minute. And God,
with that sense of humor He's famous for,
turned her into a pillar of salt, ha-ha.
Then Lot and his two sexy daughters
dug into a cave, where they all got drunk,
and there, in the godly stink of brimstone, enjoyed
a little incest, and the two girls
both gave birth to sons. Or brothers, depending
on how you look at it. And Lot had sons,
or grandsons, suit yourself, and that's
all I'm going to say about that family. I mean,

if you put this in a book,
nobody in his right mind would believe it.

But whenever I think of Sodom . . . Well,
what had those people done that was so bad,
anyway—some dice and booze,
some frisky girls, willing boys,
a little fooling around—I know
it's not exactly orthodox, but
to kill them all? To peel
the cooked flesh off those one-year-olds,
just learning their first words?
All I can say is,
God must have a weird set of values,
and if there's a Judgment Day,
as some folks think,
He's going to have a lot to answer for.

SENSUAL MUSIC

what is past, or passing, or to come
—W. B. YEATS

You know that from day one you start
to lose a little of your heart;
your mother, with a world to save,
has given birth beside a grave,
and time, relentless surgeon's knife,
year by year trims off your life.
But moments teach you not to be
deceived by immortality:
it's far too little, far too much.
What you have is what you touch;
passion feeds on bread and bells,
a chime of sounds, bouquet of smells,
someone's arm around your waist,
the best desire you'll ever taste;
and every glance is one step of
the pilgrimage that leads to love—
silver voices, golden bough:
the immortality of now.

OUR TREE

When we dug it out, thirty summers back,
it wasn't as thick as a wrist, but it was straight,
symmetrical: a hard maple
with good genes.
Small as it was, with its little world of dirt,
it took four of us to lug it back
along the river bank, to shade
the shy grass at a brand-new house.
Once in our ground, as the Bible says,
it was nothing but chattel:
we owned it.

Now paint is scabbing off the house,
and rust is cancer in the eaves again,
but the tree is tall and full
and tropically green. Two of us
who carried that sapling home
are underground forever; the other two
are going gray and making out their wills.
The maple sees it all: every year
it takes a deep breath, puffs
a thousand wings, and murmurs in the breeze:
> *There, you flesh-and-bloods who thought you owned me,*
> *my seeds are dancing over fields and meadows,*
> *and when you're lying low and making earth,*
> *I'll send up sturdy shoots around your graves.*

GERTRUDE

Gertrude Appleman, 1901–1976

God is all-knowing, all-present, and almighty.
—A CATECHISM OF CHRISTIAN DOCTRINE

I wish that all the people
who peddle God
could watch my mother die:
could see the skin and
gristle weighing only
seventy-nine, every stubborn
pound of flesh a small
death.

I wish the people who peddle God
could see her young,
lovely in gardens and
beautiful in kitchens, and could watch
the hand of God slowly
twisting her knees and fingers
till they gnarled and knotted, settling in
for thirty years of pain.

I wish the people who peddle God
could see the lightning
of His cancer stabbing
her, that small frame
tensing at every shock,
her sweet contralto scratchy with
the Lord's infection: *Philip,*
I want to die.

I wish I had them gathered round,
those preachers, popes, rabbis,

imams, priests—every
pious shill on God's payroll—and I
would pull the sheets from my mother's brittle body,
and they would fall on their knees at her bedside
to be forgiven all their
faith.

ANNIVERSARY

Maybe it wasn't strange to find
drums and cymbals where
there might have been violins, maybe
we couldn't have known; besides,
would it have mattered?
See what the years have left behind:
a thick scar in the palm of my hand,
a ragged one running along the arm.
And you:
I know your scars at midnight
by touch.

Everything we've learned, we've picked up
by ear, a pidgin language
of the heart, just
enough to get by on:
we know the value of cacophony, how to measure
with a broken yardstick,
what to do with bruised fruit.
Reading torn maps, we always
make it home, riding
on empty.

And whatever this is we've built together,
we remember sighting it skew, making it plumb
eventually, and here it stands,
stone over rock. In the walls
there are secret passages
leading to music nobody else can hear,
earthlight nobody else can see. And somewhere

in a room that's not yet finished
there are volumes in our own hand, telling
troubled tales, promises kept, and
promises
still to keep.

THE TRICKLE-DOWN THEORY OF HAPPINESS

Out of heaven, to bless the high places,
it falls on the penthouses, drizzling
at first, then a pelting allegro,
and Dick and Jane skip to the terrace
and go boogieing through the azaleas,
while mommy and daddy come running
with pots and pans, glasses, and basins
and try to hold all of it up there,
but no use, it's too much, it keeps coming,
and pours off the edges, down limestone
to the pitchers and pails on the ground, where
delirious residents catch it,
and bucket brigades get it moving
inside, until bathtubs are brimful,
but still it keeps coming, that shower
of silver in alleys and gutters,
all pouring downhill to the sleazy
red brick, and the barefoot people
who romp in it, laughing, but never
take thought for tomorrow, all spinning
in a pleasure they catch for a moment;
so when Providence turns off the spigot
and the sky goes as dry as a prairie,
then daddy looks down from the penthouse,
down to the streets, to the gutters,
and his heart goes out to his neighbors,
to the little folk thirsty for laughter,
and he prays in his boundless compassion:
on behalf of the world and its people
he demands of his God, *give me more.*

LAST-MINUTE MESSAGE FOR A TIME CAPSULE

I have to tell you this, whoever you are:
that on one summer morning here, the ocean
pounded in on tumbledown breakers,
a south wind, bustling along the shore,
whipped the froth into little rainbows,
and a reckless gull swept down the beach
as if to fly were everything it needed.
I thought of your hovering saucers,
looking for clues, and I wanted to write this down,
so it wouldn't be lost forever—
that once upon a time we had
meadows here, and astonishing things,
swans and frogs and luna moths
and blue skies that could stagger your heart.
We could have had them still,
and welcomed you to earth, but
we also had the righteous ones
who worshiped the True Faith, and Holy War.
When you go home to your shining galaxy,
say that what you learned
from this dead and barren place is
to beware the righteous ones.

BILDAD

I know what they're saying
under their breath, behind my back,
men in the sweaty bazaar,
women at the well near sundown. "He's
a tent flap in the wind," they're saying.
"His knots have come loose. Bildad
can't walk and count goats at the same time."
Well, let them talk. We knew
what we were doing, Zophar,
Eliphaz, and I, we knew our minds,
our duty, our holy obligation.
So we sat with Job for seven days
and seven nights, for his own good.
What, after all,
was in it for us but righteousness,
piety, the love of God—a God as good
and kind and loving and just
as *we* were?

Job was our friend, so when we heard
how his thousands of sheep and camels and oxen
were carried off, his children slaughtered,
servants put to the sword,
his body blistered with boils,
and only his wife still alive
to scald him with her constant
"Curse God and die"—
why naturally we had to come and sit with him,
there in the ashes. He was a mess,
frankly—those festering sores,
his head shaved ragged, his robe in tatters,

and he smelled like a day-old fish—
but what's all that among friends?

We wanted to let him talk first,
so we waited. And waited.
After those seven long days he finally spoke:
"God breaks me like a tempest.
He wounds me without cause."

That's when our sacred mission began:
"Job, you've got it all wrong,
God doesn't punish the innocent.
Think, deep in your heart,
where you've sinned, but don't
blame the Lord."
That shook him up, his eyes
darting around at us like someone
looking for a way to run.
"But I *am* innocent!" he whined.
We all had to smile,
and he jabbered on, "The arrows of the Almighty
are poisoning me. Let the day perish
when I was born . . ."
We shut him off, before his self-pity
stuck to our skin like pitch.
"Job! A hypocrite's hope
is a spiderweb, a flower in the withering sun,
its roots in stone—but the good Lord
will not cast away a perfect man."

Oh, we had him all right,
locked in logic.
He twisted and turned, and hassled us
with more of his graveyard metaphor:
"Man that is born of woman," he wailed,

"cometh forth like a flower
and is cut down. Man dieth
and riseth not. If God's scourge
kills the innocent, He
will sit there and laugh . . ."

We stopped him short. "Job,
the light of the wicked
shall be put out, the hypocrite
perish, the meat in his bowels
turned to gall, he shall vomit up
his ill-gotten riches,
he shall suck the poison of asps, burn
fire in his private places. So
confess—you must have stripped
the naked of their clothing,
sent widows away empty-handed, broken
the arms of orphans. Almighty God
is just. Confess. *Confess*."

I tell you we had him. Our syllogism
was airtight: since God is just,
He cannot torment
an innocent man;
the conclusion was as clear
as a desert sky. Job
must be guilty.

But then God opened His mouth
and in a whirlwind of rage
blasted our beautiful logic.
Out of a dust storm it came, that booming
irrelevance: "Where were you
when I made the earth, the stars,
the sea? Do you know the breadth of the world,

the treasures of the snow?
Out of whose womb comes the ice?
Can you send down the lightning?"
And more of the same, all meaning—
Why do you bother Me with your sniveling,
you insignificant maggot?
"Will you condemn Me," roared
the grimy whirlwind, "so you can be righteous?"

Some scene, isn't it? There we are,
making sense of things, putting Job in his place,
proving the neat connection between
crime and punishment—and just as our triumph
burns in Job's bewildered eyes,
God horns in with that scandalous
non sequitur. "No," He says,
"You don't suffer because you sin.
You suffer because I say so."

And Job, humble at last in spirit
as he already was in body, groveled in dirt:
"I abhor myself, Lord—I repent
in dust and ashes."

That did it. God
was finally satisfied, and Job
got his reward: his camels back,
doubled, his sheep and oxen, too, and now
his wife is pregnant, a brand-new bundle
on its way. As I always say,
toadying is good for business. Still,
this whole affair
was just cosmic whimsy, and
who needs it? That's why I don't care
when the locals whisper behind my back
and call me crazy.

But I've got children, too. Who's
going to explain this
celestial farce
to them? All I can hope now is
that Job will be utterly forgotten, and
that God's awful pronouncement
will be buried in Job's grave.
It's hard enough to bring up a family
in these troubled times without admitting
that almighty God has the morals
of a Babylonian butcher.

NIGHT THOUGHTS

Black on black, from Maine to California:
the starshine is too precious now to keep.
I'm staking all my luck on one more morning
while everyone I love is sound asleep.

Suppose tomorrow were the last clear dawning,
painting the sky with glimmers of desire,
the last pale cloud, the last bright eagle soaring,
before the final blossoming of fire—

the last green pine, and one more blue wave breaking,
the long farewell in one last robin's song,
teaching us the keenest kind of aching,
to love that well which we must leave 'ere long.

They'd feel it come in Washington and China:
the poison rain, the murder in the snow,
endless winter, birdless and benighted,
and sickness in the fields, where nothing grows.

From Paumanok it's black to the Pacific:
a nightbird says too late, you're in too deep.
Red telephones are jangling their dark traffic,
while everyone I love is sound asleep.

DAVID

After my smooth stone crushed
his head, I hacked at the throat
with his own great sword
and dragged back my ugly trophy,
oozing blood. Then
came the rout and the sexy slaughter—
I gave the guts of Philistine boys
to the buzzards and beasts
of the earth. Our women
sang in the streets, "O Saul
has slain his thousands, but David
his tens of thousands."
        I am David, I am mighty,
        and behold, the Lord is with me.

For my promised wife Michal, King Saul
demanded the foreskins of
one hundred Gentiles. I made instead
two hundred weeping widows
and cast those gory flaps
at the feet of the king, amid praises.
And God said, "I will deliver all
the Philistines into thy hands."
So I smote them hip and thigh,
and we spitted every man,
and buried our tools and our knives
in the soft flesh of their women, blood
sticky under our feet, the skulls of their children
smashed in our holy crusade.
No one escaped the justice of our God.
        I am David, I am mighty,
        and behold, the Lord is with me.

I took Michal, daughter of Saul,
to be my wife and lover;

I took Abigail, a widow,
to be my wife and lover;
and then Ahinoam
to be my wife and lover;
then Maacah and Abital
and Haggith and Eglah,
to be my wives and lovers—
and concubines without number.
But when I saw Bathsheba, no one
could satisfy me till I had her.
So, being king, I had her,
and murdered her faithful husband. Then
our gloomy local prophet
said unto me, "Thou art David,
and God hath put away
thy sin." In a tumult
of joy I smashed and burned
the ancient city of Rabbah
and made slaves and concubines
of all its godless people
who live without the blessings
of the Law.
        I am David, I am mighty,
        and behold, the Lord is with me.

Now the waves of death are upon me,
and I call upon the Lord:
the foundations of heaven move,
and smoke streams from His nostrils.
He thunders from the heavens
and rewards me much, according
to my righteousness, for
I have kept the laws of God.
He hath made all my ways to be perfect.
        I am David, I was mighty,
        and behold, the Lord is with me.

WATCHING HER SLEEP

On her left side, her right arm pillowed,
the breathing regular as waves:
it's summertime, and childhood,
her father come to life
to smooth her hair and stroll the grassy
sidewalk toward the sundaes at Prince Castle.
Coming home alone she flies
inches off the ground and finds her mother
saying go to sleep—it almost wakes her—
a quarter turn, worry in the forehead,
then the steady breathing.
No one thinks it odd she's outdoors
naked—once again
the streets are full of dimes.
But when our early neighbor
starts the mower, she
can't see where she's going
in the dark, something huge
chases her along a stone wall,
falling, falling . . .
She fights for breath,
flops over, blinks at daylight.
The warmth of arms is my reward
for the gallantry of simply
being there.

GIFTS

A winter birthday:
deep freeze out of the Yukon,
a battery dead as a dinosaur,
and an icy *Times,* its everyday smudge
full of the world as usual—famine,
murder, nukes, and the government still busy
taking bread from poets to feed the generals.
I'm finding it hard to remember when
life was a three-ring circus, all August
and sunshine and cotton candy. I do remember
that on my eighth birthday I wrote a poem
rhyming snowman and popcorn and clown,
and that very summer I saw my first circus:
poetry makes things happen.
The birds and the beasts were there, lions
in yellow cages, like animal crackers,
elephants doing their soft-shoe, and
in that magic circle,
monkeys riding clowns riding horses.
When they picked out kids
to join the parade, I found myself
grasping a mane, and flying—and afterward
two sequined beauties kissed my cheeks,
painting me up like a symbol. No wonder, then,
juggling a lifetime, I
felt the frost at midnight,
watched the woods fill up with snow,
and as the windchill dropped
to twenty below this morning,
warmed my hands at the darling buds of May,
at mermaids singing each to each,
at a magic circle where there are
no nukes or famines or tricky politicians,

but troubadours in motley doing cartwheels,
and bards on unicycles testing the high wire,
and minstrels in cap and bells taming the lions, brave
high-flying poets, all my sisters
and brothers, ready to blow out their candles
and make the same wish again, nothing extravagant,
only,
in their sponge rubber noses and polka dots,
to sing forever.

JONAH

You remember the old story,
a fisherman bragging about the one
that got away: "This big," he says,
"*this big* it was, you never saw such a fish."
"No," says the other guy, "and neither did you."
It was that kind of day—on the run
from God, I stowed away
on the S.S. *Tarshish,* got
dry-heave sick in a wicked wind,
dreaded for hours the creaky tub
would sink the lot of us, finally
got flung overboard by panicky sailors
like so much ballast, and then,
after all that, to see this monster
come bearing down on me like I was
breakfast—oh,
you can see why I've been a little fuzzy
ever since. Was I really inside—
like people are saying now—I mean
really inside that fish, or whale,
or whatever it was, every eyewitness
gives you a different story—anyway,
was I *really*
in the belly of that thing
for three whole days?

I know what you're thinking—
"If *you* don't know, who does?" That's
what you're thinking, isn't it? Well,
don't get smug, this
is stickier than you think.
You've had those days, don't tell me you haven't—
you brush the cobwebs out of your eyes,

cursing the sunrise,
and there's that big jug
sitting there empty, and you say, my God,
did I drink it all? And the truth is,
you don't remember. It's like that.
I do remember this big mouth coming at me
like a tidal wave, and the next thing I know
it's three days later, and I'm on the beach,
hungry as a seagull and ready to kill
for a mug of the good stuff. But
what exactly had happened?

I know there's this rumor going around
that I was inside that fish, but wait
a minute, look at my skin—
all in one piece. How
could I have been swallowed and not been
chewed up, or at least munched on a little? Or
suppose I did somehow get gulped down whole,
and didn't break my neck going through
that churning gullet, then
what did I do for air for three days,
down there with all those squid and dead herring?
Just try to picture that scene,
as I do all the time now—
swimming in belly-soup, seasick whenever
the beast does its foraging dance,
and when it cranks up its digestive machine,
the squid and I get sprayed
with acid strong enough
to eat away my sandals.
And maybe the whale, or whatever it was,
gets lucky, hits a school
of irresistible tidbits,
and all of a sudden I'm dumped on by a ton

of fresh mackerel.
Am I supposed to believe
I survived all that for three days
and three nights, the gristly stomach
grinding away at everything inside,
squeezing me to mush? Oh,
come on!

Look, if you're so crazy
about the fish story, I've got a lot
of others you'd like—maybe
the one where Moses' staff turns into a snake,
or the time he splits the Red Sea like an apple,
or when Joshua knocks down a stone wall
by yelling at it,
or when Samson kills a thousand armed men
with a piece of bone—say,
I could go on and on. And if
you swear to me you swallow all that,
I mean really absolutely believe it
at high noon on a sunny summer day,
then maybe I'll think again about
swallowing the whale.

FLEAS

I form the light, and create darkness:
I make peace, and create evil:
I the Lord do all these things.

—ISAIAH 45:7

I think that I shall never see
a poem as ugly as a flea,
a flea whose hungry mouth is pressed
against a buttock or a breast,
a flea that spreads disease all day
and lifts its little claws to prey:
poems are made by you and me,
but only God can make a flea.

I think that no one ever made
a poem as powerful as AIDS,
or plagues that may in summer kill
half the bishops in Brazil
and share the good Lord's Final Answer
with clots and cholera and cancer—
for God concocted pox to mock us,
staph and syph and streptococcus:
poems are made by bards or hacks,
but only God makes cardiacs.

I think that I shall never smell
a poem as pungent as a hell,
where grinning devils turn the screws
on saintly Sikhs and upright Jews,
giving them the holy scorcher,
timeless, transcendental torture:
poems can make you want to yell,
but only God can give you hell.

BEFORE YOU PUSH THE RED BUTTON

You need to know what it is,
what it really is that you're doing, so
there are certain requirements.

One: take a razor blade and make a slit
through your fingernail, from the cuticle
out to the edge; then two more slits, one
on each side.

Two: pick up the pliers and grip firmly
one of the strips of fingernail
and pull it off, all the way off,
allowing for the extra resistance
at the root. Do the same
to the other three strips, then proceed
to the next nail. It may not be easy at first,
but be firm. Pushing the red button, after all,
isn't kid stuff.

Three: when that hand is finished, do the other.
You'll notice that you never really
get used to the fine
texture of ripping flesh, so
take a ten-minute break, then

Four: do the toes. At last
you're beginning to understand
the red button; you have some pale
impression of a winter
of mutilations, a desert of epitaphs.
One more thing:
for anyone with a red button
who happens to be a slow learner,
there are other requirements, involving
Five / Six / Seven: the tongue / the eyeballs /
the genitals.

AND THEN THE PERFECT TRUTH OF HATRED

There was a preacher in our town
whose Sunday text was the Prince of Peace,
but
when he looked out at the Monday world—
at the uppity blacks and pushy Jews
and sassy wives and sneaky heathen—blood
scalded his face as purple as if
he'd hung by his heels. Then
his back-yard, barber-shop, street-corner sermons
scorched us with all the omens of siege:
our roofs aflame, tigers at the gates,
hoodlums pillaging homes, ravaging
wives and daughters, the sky
come crashing down,
and we gazed into his blazing truth
of Onward Christian Soldiers,
A Mighty Fortress Is Our God,
Soldiers of the Cross. No question now
of sissy charity, this
was the Church Militant, burning
its lightning bolts across
our low horizons.

It's been a while since that preacher went off
to the big apartheid in the sky,
and the only hint of eternal life
is the way he resurrects each week
to sell salvation on the screen.
He's younger after all these years,
in designer suits and toothy smiles,
but we know him by the cunning eyes
where he harbors his old stooges,
Satan, Jehovah. He calls them up,

and across the country, glands begin
pumping bile into our lives:
sleet storms in the voice,
cords in the neck like bullwhips,
broken promises, broken bones—
the wreckage of his deep
sincerity.

MARY

Years later, it was, after everything
got hazy in my head—those buzzing flies,
the gossips, graybeards, hustling evangelists—
they wanted facts, they said,
but what they were really after
was miracles.
Miracles, imagine! I was only a girl
when it happened, Joseph
acting edgy and claiming
it wasn't his baby . . .

Anyway, years later
they wanted miracles, like the big-time cults
up in Rome and Athens, God
come down in a shower of coins,
a sexy swan, something like that.
But no, there was only
one wild-eyed man at our kitchen window
telling me I'm lucky.
And pregnant.
I said, "Talk sense, mister, it's got to be
the one thing or the other."
No big swans, no golden coins
in that grubby mule-and-donkey village. Still,
they wanted miracles,
and what could I tell them? He
was my baby, after all, I washed
his little bum, was I
supposed to think I was wiping
God Almighty?

But they *wanted miracles,* kept after me
to come up with one: "This fellow at the window,

did he by any chance have wings?"
"Wings! Do frogs have wings?
Do camels fly?"
They thought it over. "Cherubim," they said,
"may walk the earth like men
and work their wonders."
I laughed in their hairy faces. No
cherub, that guy! But
they wouldn't quit—fanatics, like
the gang *he* fell in with years ago,
all goading him till he began to believe
in quick cures and faith-healing,
just like the cranks in Jerusalem, every
phony in town speaking in tongues
and handling snakes. Not exactly
what you'd want for your son, is it?
I tried to warn him, but he just says,
"I must be about my father's business."
"Fine, " I say, "I'll buy you a new
hammer." But nothing could stop him, already
hooked on the crowds, the hosannas,
the thrill of needling the bureaucrats.
Holier than thou, he got, roughing up
the rabbis even. Every night
I cried myself to sleep—my son,
my baby boy . . .

You know how it all turned out, the crunch
of those awful spikes,
the spear in his side, the whole town watching,
home-town folks come down from Nazareth
with a strange gleam in their eyes. Then later on
the grave robbers, the hucksters, the imposters all
claiming to be him. I was sick

for a year, his bloody image
blurring the sunlight.

And now they want miracles, God
at my maidenhead, sex without sin.
"Go home," I tell them, "back to your libraries,
read about your fancy Greeks,
and come up with something amazing, if you must."

Me, I'm just a small-town woman,
a carpenter's wife, Jewish mother, nothing
special. But listen,
whenever I told my baby a fairy tale,
I let him know it was a fairy tale.
Go, all of you, and do likewise.

CREDO

I am modern. And educated. And reasonable.
And I believe in Jesus Christ, son
of the living God.
When they tell me He
was born of a virgin, I say, well,
it's unusual, of course, but in the arms of God,
anything is possible . . .
When they tell me that a bright new star
appeared in the eastern sky,
shining over His manger, I say, well,
I know it's not customary
to improvise stars like that, but remember,
we set up searchlights now, just
to open a used-car lot, and after all,
this *is* the Son of God, isn't it? . . .
They tell me He cast out demons,
and I say, well,
you have to understand the peculiar idiom
of a given historical time . . .
They tell me His voice could calm a tempest,
and I reflect on all the unexplained
phenomena
of our physical world . . .
They tell me His touch cured blindness,
made the lame walk, the lepers clean,
and brought corpses back to life—
and I'm reminded of the psychic component
of so much modern medicine . . .
They tell me He fed five thousand
with five loaves and two fishes,
that He walked on the surface of the sea,
that He rose from the dead—

and I relish the poetic truth
of those venerable symbols.

In the backward villages of Asia,
the gods have as many limbs
as spiders, and take on monstrous forms
as quickly as a cloud. The natives,
shrouded in their age-old ignorance
and superstition, believe
the most bizarre tales about them,
despite the best efforts
of our enlightened missionaries.

COAST TO COAST

The bird that shook the earth at J.F.K.
goes blind to milkweed, riverbanks, the wrecks
of elm trees full of liquor and decay—
and jars the earth again at L.A.X.

Once, on two-lane roads, our crazy drives
across the country tallied every mile
in graves or gardens: glimpses in our lives
to make the busy continent worthwhile.

Friendly, then, the smell of woods and fields,
the flash of finches and the scud of crows,
the rub of asphalt underneath our wheels
as tangible as sand between the toes.

From orchards out to prairies, then to cactus,
the rock and mud and clay were in our bones:
as birches turned to oak, then eucalyptus,
we learned our lover's body stone by stone.

Now, going home we're blind again, seven
miles above the earth on chartered wings:
in a pressurized and air-conditioned heaven
the open road's a song nobody sings.

JUDAS

Ask Peter, ask Paul—the really unbearable part
was figuring out those hillbilly parables.
We understood the straight stuff, "Blessed
are the peacemakers," and such, but not
those constant "It is like unto's . . ."
They always sent shivers through us—we knew
there'd be catechism after the sermon.
"It is like unto sowing seeds," he'd say
in that Nazarene country drawl,
"some of them fall on good soil,
others on rock." Well, everybody knows that,
but what did he mean by it?
He'd only say, "Who hath ears to hear,
let him hear." Big help.
Or he'd say, "It is like unto a mustard seed
that grows into a huge plant." Mmm-hmm.
He'd say, "The kingdom of heaven
is like unto leaven," and so on.
And then, of course, that inevitable
"Who hath ears to hear," etcetera.
We were always as nervous as cats in a doghouse,
John sneaking glances at James, James
dragging his toe in the sand and looking
at Thomas, Thomas looking doubtful,
all of us hoping that someone would understand.
But we never did, not one single time—finally
he always had to explain. "The *field*
is the *world*," he'd say, his eyebrows grim
as a tax collector, "The good seed
are the children of the kingdom, get it?"
Oh, sure, it's easy when you already
know the answer, but
suppose it'd been you, hearing

for the hundredth time
those words like needles in your nerves,
"It is like unto, it is like unto . . ."
It drives you over the edge, finally, even
Peter claiming he didn't know him,
and I . . . Well,
with or without those thirty pieces of silver,
it's a wonder that none of the others
crossed him first.

HEADING NORTH

Day breaks
your heart: pack
the smell of tanning oil
beside your snorkels and
whip your bones to a raw
future, dragging along
the pain of orchids and
hibiscus. Home again,
fighting your way through slush,
you are condemned to memories
of angelfish in coral reefs,
dazzling your frosted eyeballs. Now
your slurred footsteps
won't beat the walk light; nothing
the color of palm trees blossoms
on Tenth Street. Wake, if you must,
to half-hour delays
in the morning rush, prophecies
of turmoil in the sky,
minutes carefully pieced together
for the sake of a thousand nothings. But
dream, in your bickering taxis,
of the slow wake of white sails,
your purest vision turning in
upon itself, leaving
everything to chance except
your life:
the sun on your pale back,
the lust of ocean along your skin,
a lifetime that's finally worth it
every time you breathe.

MARTHA

Martha Haberkorn, 1899–1983

Imagine her moving from sink to stove,
from need to need,
planting seeds, baking cakes,
visiting shut-ins,
and on Sundays glittering
with stained glass, hearing always
the praises of a jealous God,
and every night His fierce voice
hissing, "Listen, listen,
> a fire is kindled in mine anger
> and shall burn unto the lowest hell,
> and sinners shall be devoured
> with burning heat and with bitter destruction,
> the teeth of beasts, the poison of serpents,
> the sword without, and terror within,
> to Me belongeth vengeance."
Thus
spake the Lord.

So when the bad times came to her troubled mind
and she bore the modern torture of her pills
and the ancient menace of the lakes of fire,
and every night came on in a black torment,
then the Lord was faithful to her bed,
reminding her in the dangerous hours
of all the evil things she'd ever done—
the omissions, the white lies, the private
secrets locked away—little
derelictions from
her eighty-four years of goodness.
And God would not relent
when her body trembled

and her words came in gargling
whispers—when, in the dark chambers
of the heart, the pounding
was hammers on nerve-ends—the sword without,
the terror within—and a tiny voice
grieved her guilty life:
"I've done so many bad things, and now
Jesus won't forgive me, the Lord
won't let me rest."

How can we then forgive this God
who will not forgive His saints?
We are here to witness
that the sins of the Lord are past pardon.
He is therefore banished from our planet
to shuffle through a universe of stars,
while the tree of knowledge sows its golden apples
all across this land.

LIGHTING YOUR BIRTHDAY CAKE

Of course we didn't come this far
without leaving a trail, but it's only
footprints on a beach: one wash
through our memories, and it's gone. Strange,
so much passion, commitment, doomed
to be drifted over like
Troy and Babylon, pitiful echoes now
of all those eager heartbeats.
You've always cared so much,
about us, sure, but really everything—
hungry kids, dolphins, over-
population, and the old foes: batterers, bishops,
gunslingers, chauvinists—nothing escapes
your rage or compassion; earthquakes in Asia
shake our midnight bedroom. You always knew
that the bright bird of sympathy
is the only godliness on earth,
hovering over these grubby streets
on better wings than angels'. Now
I can't believe in a world without
your bonfire of outrage, small flame of anguish,
pink glow of happiness.
Remember how I need your warmth:
as you blow out these candles, make a wish
to keep the fires burning.

JESUS

We're cast in the image of God,
they say, but
up here the image blurs—
that Pharisee at the edge of the crowd,
the one with a burro's belly
and a toad's complexion—
is he the real thing, God
in the flesh?
Or maybe that saintly starveling, all
bones in her pinched piety—does God
have a profile like hers?

Just days ago, these very faces,
rainbowed with joy, saw palm trees
ripped and strewn for the son of man. Now
my palms are red,
and it's all changed—bloodlust
smudges the thousand grins
of God. Here
in this Friday frenzy, just
look at them, the veins
in that legionnaire's legs, the brutal
mouth, the pocked face, and . . .
And of course the handsome boy out there
eyeing the splendid line
of that girl's arm—them, too.
It all counts,
doesn't it?

I suppose they aren't even wondering,
this godly rabble out for fun,
expecting something big today, something
spectacular. So I should be telling them,

now, before I'm dust forever—
you don't pay off an ugly squint
with a nice ankle; a luscious
lower lip doesn't make up
for a running sore; and above all, nobody
ever promised you justice.
All you have to know is
that a beautiful shoulder is God, but
a twisted leg is God, too,
and crooked noses and bad teeth. This
is the real revelation—that God
is only a trick with mirrors, our
dark reflection in a glass.

So up here, getting this panoramic view,
I hear the voices of God on every side,
all mocking me, "Hold on,
it's your big scene!" And I cry out
to every smooth and sacred cheek,
to every holy wart and pustule—the spikes
tearing at my hands—I call to every
body on this hill of skulls,
Why?
Why have you
forsaken me?

BUT THE DAISIES WILL NOT BE DECEIVED BY THE GODS

Seductions as countless as crosses,
as icons, none of it ever
surprising, not even
the stare of the sky
keeping score. The prize for yielding,
for giving in to paradise,
is laying down the awful burden
of mind: surrender
rings from the steeples and calls
from the minarets and temples.
But challenges sing
in the sway of treetops,
in the flutter of sparrows,
in chirring and stalking,
in waking and ripening—let
there be light enough, and
everywhere backbone stiffens
in saplings and clover. Praises, then,
to sunfish and squirrels,
blessings to bugs. Turning our backs
on the bloody altars,
we cherish each other, living here
in this brave world
with our neighbors, the earthworms,
and our old friends, the ferns
and the daisies.

KISSING THE ABORIGINES
(Kakadu)

Fire in your veins: the sun smolders
under your skin. Bare in the shimmer,
they fold their dusty legs and drum
on hollow logs a blistering
of kangaroo and crocodile heat,
sounding the cadences of dream,
a journey to endless midnight. Now
the glistening bodies rise to touch you,
faces painted the color of hope.
Black and white skins meet in a fever,
wet lips mark your life with an X,
and you suddenly know the songs of your people,
the dances. Bush runs wild in your gristle,
dingoes howl in the caves of your skull.
Never again in your ancient life
will you see so far, so clearly.

THEM

> *We all have enough strength to bear*
> *the misfortunes of others.*
>
> —LA ROCHEFOUCAULD

Rush hour
on the Downtown Express: victims
splintered into halftones, buried
in the times, a thousand tiny dots.
      At 59th Street: blood
      on the Golden Pagoda.
      42nd Street: slaughter
      in the Blue Mosque.
      34th: the shattered roofs
      of synagogues.
      14th: corpses in the rubble
      of churches.
A throng of little dots, dancing
in front of your mask:
other people's pain.

But look, the dots have broken loose
and are swarming like bees, attacking
the woman whose sleeve is touching yours,
wearing a mask exactly like her face—
and now she's out of control,
breaking the rules, tearing off the mask,
and she cries with the screaming of stallions,
barbarian yells, wind in the howling ruins.

And busy people glance out of their eyeholes
and frown
and bury themselves
in the times.

EULOGY

That swain in Shakespeare, penning ballads
to his lady's eyebrow: if just once
he could have seen my sweetheart's breasts,
he would have written epics. Oh,
they are so springtime-sweet and summer-lilting,
those twin blossoms, I should have found
a painter intimate with tender shades
of pink and cream
to immortalize their harmony.

Because
up there on the seventh floor
they are cutting one of them away,
the one we touched last week and felt
the poisoned pearl.
Now the knives are working, working,
I feel them stabbing through my flesh.
She will come back gray, remembering
to smile, the bandages weeping blood,
her beauty scarred,
her life saved.

I will love her more
than yesterday.

DAYS ONE THROUGH SIX, ETC.

You keep on asking me that—
"Which day was the hardest?"
Blockheads! They were *all* hard.
And of course, since I'm omnipotent,
they were all easy.
It was Chaos, to begin with. Can you imagine
Primeval Chaos? Of course you can't.
How long had it been swirling around out there?
Forever.
How long had *I* been there?
Longer than that.
It was a mess, that's what it was. Chaos is
rocky. Fuzzy. Slippery. Prickly.
As scraggly and obstreperous as the endless behind
of an infinite jackass. Shove on it anywhere,
it gives, then slips in behind you,
like smog, like lava, like slag.
I'm telling you, chaos is—*chaotic.*
You see what I was up against. Who
could make a world out of that muck?
I could, that's who—land
from water, light from dark, and so on.
It might seem like a piece of cake
now that it's done, but
back then, without a blueprint,
without a set of instructions, without a committee,
could *you* have created a *firmament?*

Of course there were bugs in the process,
grit in the gears, blips, bloopers—
bringing forth grass and trees on Day Three
and not making sunlight until Day Four, that,
I must say, wasn't my best move.

And making the animals and vegetables before
there was any rain whatsoever—well,
anyone can have a bad day.
Even Adam, as it turned out, wasn't such a great
idea—those shifty eyes, the alibis,
blaming things on his wife—I mean,
it set a bad example. How could he
expect that little toddler, Cain,
to learn correct family values
with a role model like him?
And then there was the nasty squabble
over the beasts and birds.
OK, I admit I told Adam
to name them, but—Platypus?
Aardvark? Hippopotamus?
Let me make one thing perfectly clear—
he didn't get that gibberish from *Me.*
No, I don't need a planet to fall on Me,
I know something about subtext.
He did it to irritate Me, just plain
spite—and did I need the aggravation?
Well, as you know, things went from bad
to worse, from begat to begat,
father to son, the evil fruit
of all that early bile. So next
there was narcissism, then bigotry,
then jealousy, rage, *vengeance!*
And finally I realized, the spawn of Adam
had become exactly like—Me.

No Deity with any self-respect
would tolerate that kind
of competition, so what could I do?
I killed them all, that's what!
Just as the Good Book says,

I drowned man, woman, and child, like
so many cats. Oh, I saved a few
for restocking, Noah and his crew,
the best of the lot, I thought. But
now you're all back to your old tricks again,
just about due for another good ducking,
or maybe a giant barbecue.
And I'm warning you, if I have to do it again,
there won't be any survivors, not even
a cockroach! Then,
for the first time since it was Primeval
Chaos, the world will be perfect—
nobody in it but Me.

SUPERSTITION

We see only our shadows on the wall of the cave.
—PLATO

Outside
the holy winds are raging,
and here in the dusk of our lives,
patterns blur along the wall:
the games of forgotten children,
the arc of dying swallows,
wilting goldenrod—shadows now
along this barren rock.
Here, among fleeting caresses,
frenzied voices are crying *Believe,*
as our lives flare up in glory—
the gorgeous blast of shrapnel,
the halo of flashing guns—
while sages, standing in God's freezing fire,
breathe certainty, certainty,
certainty.

POSSESSED

Demons crowd your closets, reeking wool
and cotton; in your cabinets
crystal and china feed on your dark
desires; appliances, mortal
and venial, hum dirges
in your head, while downstairs
pumps and motors suck crimson
juices from your life;
and the glut of papers and disks and tapes,
and the piles of books and books and books
surround you, blocking the doorways.
Things, your things, no exorcism now,
their black wings beat hot winds
that choke you: *Mine,* they shriek,
you're mine, all mine.

HOW TO LIVE

So that's how it is, Mac—you're doing hard time
in a red brick slammer they call a school,
four years of Don't do this, Don't do that—
and your big fat reward for all that zilch
is beers and cheers in the sky when you die,
you know what I'm saying? . . .
OK, one more of the same,
and make it a double . . .
So—our whole senior year we're taking
a load of guff from this drill sergeant
in drag, who'd been to college, big deal,
but God Almighty knows when. And I guess
nobody ever slipped her the hint she wasn't
God Almighty herself—she spit out rules
like the Ten Commandments, and it was holy
hell if you crossed her. Well, there we were,
Buck and Billy and me—Young, Yates,
and Yankowitz, the Three Y's Guys, they called us.
Thanks to our pal, the alphabet,
we all end up in the rump of the room
and take turns driving Old Teach up the wall,
with my famous ten-minute sneezing routine
whenever she mentions Snake-speare,
or Buck's juicy belching to the tune
of the immortal Sheets and Kelly, nothing
serious. I mean, that's the whole point, see,
she's got no sense of humor at all.
She drags us into a swamp
of a poem nobody can wade through,
not even the nerds, and then digs in.
"Think it through," she says,
"What *is* your head, anyway, a football?"
Well, *my* head's not up my pants,

I could buy and sell her any time . . .
Sure, Mac, one more might
ease the pain . . .
Anyway, she just won't stop. "Work,"
she keeps saying, "Wasting your time
means wasting your life," and so on.
Man, I could barf in a bucket, even now.
Every single thing she makes us read
has to have a boy scout moral, like
"Keep your promises," or "Never
betray a friend," etcetera, etcetera.
What is this, anyway, Sunday School?
And half the town tags her a dirty atheist
because she never darkens a church door, not even
on Easter when all the backsliders slink in
for their annual tuneups. But what the hell,
she's preaching her own sermon every day.
So there we are, reading these moldy books,
Alfred Lord Frigging Tennis Shoe, for godsake,
or Lord Bypass, or Emily Dickhead, and she comes up
with "Know who you really are"—as if we didn't—
or her top-of-the-line, state-of-the-art,
industrial-strength zinger,
"Be responsible for yourself."
Responsible! Listen,
you don't run the biggest used-car lot in town
not knowing who's responsible, even if it means
hacking out a lot of deadwood
when they get too old to cut the mustard,
you know what I'm saying? . . .
Yeah, Mac, one more, why not? . . .
Well, Old Teach never got voted
Most Popular, that's for damn sure.
But get this—last weekend
we all dragged our butts to our very first

Mickey-Mouse class reunion. Hey,
after twenty years, that
was a laugh-and-a-half—a bunch
of balding guys and beefy broads!
Except for me, of course,
and I married the prom queen, maybe you think
those losers didn't turn green
when they saw the two of us?
So we're all sitting around, bending our elbows,
and somebody says, "I hear Old Teach
kicked the bucket a year ago." And I say,
"What was the old dump truck, anyway,
ninety-nine?" And we have a big laugh, and then
some bubblehead says, "You know, it's funny, but
I learned a lot from Old Teach."
And another clown pipes up, "Yeah,
come to think of it, I did, too."
And pretty soon the whole damn table
is nodding away, and one of the bimbos is sniffling,
and I say, "Hey, what is this,
we talking about the old gray mare or not,
I mean, are you guys gonna feed me some of
her fruit salad now, an airy-fairy
rhyme or two?" But they all just sit there
like pallbearers, and one guy—Donald,
the kinkiest little creep in the whole class—
he says, "Nah, Jerry, that ain't it."
And everybody nods again like a bunch
of dingalings, and now I'm getting
a little aggravated, and I say,
"So what the *hell*, then?"
And Donald says, "It wasn't the books
and the rhymes exactly. I guess she just
taught me how to live."
Jeeeesus! I laugh till I split! This flyspeck,

this walking disease who just spent twenty years
pushing boxes in a warehouse—I could buy and sell
the guy, you know what I'm saying? And *he's* giving *us*
the scoop? *He* knows how to *live?*
But nobody else is laughing,
and the sniffling cow has her hanky out,
and I think about all that baloney—"Think
it through," "Know who you really are,"
and I have to laugh again. Christ,
nobody ever made a buck on *that* . . .
Yeah, Mac, one for the road, then
I gotta get back to the old lady
or catch hell again tonight. What a *crock*—
prom queen twenty years ago,
wild as a weed, and now, six kids later,
she's nonstop bellyaching—
more like Old Teach every day.
"How to *live?*" Hey, Buddy,
take a look at me—
I got wise to *that* one, years ago.

GRAVITY

F=Gmm'/r²: directly proportional to the product
of the masses, inversely proportional to the square
of the distance . . .

One false step and you're off the ladder,
plunging in free-fall   through
a lifetime   proportional
to the product of its losses   down
through decades to Mother Earth   who breaks
your heart   your spirit   your bones
jarring your life into ceaseless   pain.

And the pain that will not stop
is a poison vine, its roots deep in your chest,
is a snake reaming your veins, gouging out endless
yesterdays, the ceaseless pain
of history: night after night
you cannot sleep—in the dreary hours
you read about the Age of Faith,
when godly ones bowed to a holy
ghost, told their beads to a blessed mother,
and ripped off the screaming fingernails
of unbelievers; when priests, inspired
by the Pope's own personal blessing,
tore off nipples with red-hot tongs;
when monks thumbed out the eyeballs
of heretics and saints, and seared their flesh
to purify their souls.

With enough gravity and pain,
with enough pain long enough,
we will see their glowing eyes: the fervent ones
on the march again. But because our memories

are inversely proportional to
the distance between them, we don't recall
that when the high wall between priest
and politics is wrecked by frenzied mobs
screaming Hallelujah,
then the godly ones will lead us again—
our ears sliced off,
our tongues slit through,
our foreheads branded—
they will lead us triumphantly back,
back through our hazy memories,
to burn again
in an Age of Faith.

NEVER-NEVER LAND

We're smaller by the minute: yesterday
grownups, this morning teens,
an hour ago kids, and now
we're in our baby-blue pajamas,
holding pink bunnies, all ears,
the house shrunk down to our size as
we sneak through the hallway
to the top of the stairs
and peek down into yellow lamplight where
mommy and daddy are playing house,
their murmurs lullabies, making us drowsy,
and as we watch them kiss
and curl up on the sofa,
we lose our grip on furry toys,
and drift away to summer sunshine,
not knowing when they come upstairs
and pick us up and carry us like dolls
back to bed.

A PRIEST FOREVER

The first time?
So long ago—that brown-eyed boy . . .
How can I say this, Your Reverences,
so you'll understand? Maybe
it was the tilt of his pretty neck
when he pondered the mysteries—Grace,
the Trinity—the way his lower lip
curled like a petal, the way . . .
But *you* know what I mean—down
from your high pulpits and into the dirty streets—
you know there are some provocations
the good Lord made no sinew
strong enough to resist. Think
of David and Jonathan, snarled forever
in a tender web as tough as twine—
like that, maybe—like being driven
by flames, deep in the places we hide,
renounce, deny . . .

No, Monsignor, try to understand—
if your inquest here is meant
to "evaluate" me again, then
you have to feel that fever in the loins
when a child's face looks up
from the wafer-thin body of Christ, innocent eyes
flooding with wonder. You have to see
that the Lord, the good Lord,
has willed something beyond commandments,
beyond dogma, beyond law or custom,
something—irresistible . . .

All right—the first time—
of course I remember.
It was a smoldering August afternoon,
the hottest day in the history
of this whole state. And there
in the cobweb aftermath
of too many questions—what is mortal sin?
what are the dangers to chastity?—alone,
almost alone in the church, after
my little pupils had all run off
to baseball, ice cream, whatever,
he lingered on, in the dim vestry . . .

Well, if you insist, I did ask him
to stay—because,
after all those catechism lessons, there was still
one urgent question hanging
in the clammy air,
and inch by inch, among the ghostly chasubles,
we found ourselves edging closer to it.
Somehow, then, my anointed hand was blessing
his brown hair, one finger ordained to touch
the petal of that lower lip. And there
in that sweaty room—dear Jesus, how I still
feel the heat—I . . . We . . .

Yes, of course—the others. All
the others . . . But after the first time,
how do you tell them apart?
Let's see—there was a blue-eyed kid
with an angel's tongue—what was his name?
And a cherub with golden hair, who
used his indifference like a tease. And . . .
Sixty-eight of them, did you say? All
testifying to . . .

What? I? "Ruined their lives"?
Wait a minute, let's get this straight—
my passion *gave* them a life, gave them
something rich and ripe in their green youth,
something to measure all intimate flesh against,
forever. After that,
they ruined their own lives, maybe.
But with me they were full of a love
firmer than anything their meager years
had ever tasted . . .

Love, you heard me—you
with all your degrees, your tight mouths,
your clinical jargon, don't tell me
you've never had a movement below your belt
that wasn't intestinal. Listen,
this is not in Aquinas,
not in our learned encyclicals. But
there's a force that moves in our marrow,
that slithered there, long before
theology—something with ape in it,
something with the squirm of snakes,
the thrust of rams. And whatever it is,
it knows what it wants . . .

Ah—your glittering eyes
show me you understand. And your ramrod backs
tell me you'll never admit it.
But I'm not alone here, am I?
We're in this together, the same old
celibate fix—"It's better
to marry than to burn," our little
inside joke. And it all comes down
to one poor sinner in a straight-back chair
entertaining a dozen sanctimonious . . .

That word is for the record, Monsignor.
Remember the last time we met like this—
how I pleaded time, place, circumstance,
mitigating niceties, anything but the truth.
And how you enjoyed flaying me then—
you nailed me to lust like a rugged cross,
brushed aside my passion, turned your back
on my word made flesh, hoping
that no more boyish voices
would speak its name to daylight . . .

Yes, Reverends, I learned
a little something then, in all that
groveling—learned that whatever
the meek may wangle in this life,
whatever skimpy joy they manage
to snuggle up to at night, one thing
is as certain as graveyards—the meek
will never, in any shy season,
inherit the earth.
So excuse me if I don't
bob and duck this time.
You have your job to do, go ahead,
throw me to the wolves
and pay off my little lovers—
plaintiffs, have it your way—
hush them up with a million bucks
in widows' pennies. Not a bad price
for all that ecstasy . . .

Oh, I know where I'm headed—
to "therapy," as we always say,
a little paid vacation
with others who loved not wisely
but too young—and also, of course,

with the usual slew of dehydrating
whiskey priests. But don't forget
that when they say I'm "recovered" again,
they'll send me off to another parish,
with more of those little lambs—a priest,
after all, is a priest forever.
Meanwhile, as I bide my time,
and count my beads, and hum to myself
those luscious songs of Solomon,
what I'll be thinking about—
rely on this, Your Reverences—
what I'll be thinking about
is that brown-eyed boy
with the graceful neck, and the lower lip
that curled like a petal.

VASECTOMY

After the steaming bodies swept
through the hungry streets of swollen cities;
after the vast pink spawning of family
poisoned the rivers and ravaged the prairies;
after the gamble of latex and
diaphragms and pills;
I invoked the white robes, gleaming blades
ready for blood, and, feeling the scourge
of Increase and Multiply, made
affirmation: *Yes,* deliver us from
complicity.
And after the precision of scalpels,
I woke to a landscape of sunshine where
the catbird mates for life and
maps trace out no alibis—stepped
into a morning of naked truth,
where acts mean what they really are:
the purity of loving
for the sake of love.

CREATION

for the discoverer of the Grotte de Lascaux:
Marcel Ravidat, 1923–1995

On all the living walls
of this dim cave,
soot and ochre, acts of will,
come down to us to say:

This is who we were.
We foraged here in an age of ice,
and, warmed by the fur of wolves,
felt the pride of predators
going for game.
Here we painted the strength of bulls,
the grace of deer, turned life into art,
and left this testimony on our walls.
Explorers of the future, see how,
when our dreams reach forward,
your wonder reaches back, and we embrace.
When we are long since dust,
and false prophets come,
then don't forget that *we* were your creators.
So build your days
on what you know is real, and remember
that nothing will keep your lives alive
but art—the black and ochre visions
you draw inside your cave
will honor your lost tribe,
when explorers in some far future
marvel at the paintings on *your* walls.

WILL

More or less sound
of mind and memory,
I venture this testament.

1

To the poets, in the perfect pitch
of your dangerous music,
I bequeath the fiber of quench and gravel,
slush and splinter, ratchet,
forage, and fizz.
And though you will face the welter
of blizzard, tussle, and brawl, the scud
of umbrage, rankle, and jeer,
I leave you the spell
of periwinkle, condor, daffodil, velvet,
trickle, rapture, and pine.
Even in the wasteland of writer's block
and the quicksand of murderous deadlines,
you will find them sprouting up
somewhere in sunshine: impudent, racy,
passionate, irresistible.
Gather them in
with pleasure.

2

To the lovers, in the blooming
of each new moment, I hereby bequeath
a lifetime of honor and cherish.
I endow you with a glimpse of forsythia,
the shimmer of silk on a chair back,
the smell of bakeries at sunrise,
the secrets of sparrows.
And because there will be detours and chuckholes,

fields of nettles, and weeks of freezing rain,
I leave you my vested interest
in maple trees, jonquils, coral, and amber,
the flavor of raspberries, a taste of skin,
and yells of joy in troubled skies—
all of it for worse,
for better.

In witness whereof, this day
I set my hand—
and hope.

HOLDING ON
   Trieste Revisited

Knowing all about goodbye,
the sea still dreams of a reckless moon
steering a path across riot, straight
to your naked toes. And somewhere
small voices are singing,
Don't leave. Don't go. Stay with me
forever—echoes out of the starlight,
out of the lonely wrecks of galleons, out
of the eloquent earth, out of caverns
breathing bison, bulls, and deer,
out of our first goodbye
at the edge of this busy sea
brimming with pain.

   The next goodbye
   will be harder   we know
   how it will come
   like a summer squall
   there will be no warning
   it will strike at dawn
   at noon   at sunset
   a day like any
   other   but
   suddenly it's
   the last hour   before
   the white ritual
   of X rays   potions
   the quiet room . . .

Now in our rumpled sheets,
by the sleepy, whispering sea,

■ ■ ■

only ripples on the surface, but below
all mystery, and a steady murmur—
Don't leave. Don't go. Stay with me
forever.

INDEX OF TITLES

Afterward, 89

Alive, 90

And Then the Perfect Truth of Hatred, 219

Anniversary, 200

Ant, The, 151

Ars Poetica, 100

At the End of the World, 92

At the Nativity Bar and Poolroom, 29

Before You Push the Red Button, 218

Better Half, 119

Bicentennial: The Course of Empire, 61

Bildad, 203

Birthday Card to My Mother, 107

"Black-Footed Ferret Endangered," 144

But the Daisies Will Not Be Deceived by the Gods, 235

Butterwort, 40

Caravan, 78

Central Park: The Anatomy Lesson, 77

Coast to Coast, 226

Congenial Poet Desires Intense Relationship with Warm, Intelligent Poem, 109

Creation, 257

Credo, 224

Crystal Anniversary, 8

Darwin's Bestiary: Prologue, The Ant, The Worm, The Rabbit, The Gossamer, 150

David, 209

Day of the Hawk, 19

Days One through Six, etc., 239

Dolphins, 7

East Hampton: The Structure of Sound, 69

Economics, 115

Enemy, 44

Eulogy, 238

Euphorias: Waldorf-Astoria Euphoria, Hunkydoria Euphoria, 155

Eve, 175

Eye for an Eye, An, 177

Faith-Healer Speaks, The, 145

Fighting the Bureaucracy, 62

First Snow, 112

Fleas, 217

For Lucia and the Black Widows of Sperlonga, 83

Four Measures: Earth, Air, Water, Fire, 22

Gathering at the River, 173

Gertrude, 198

Gifts, 212

Girl Who Hated Threes, The, 102

Gossamer, The, 154

Gravity, 248

Hand-Ax, The, 138

Heading North, 229

Heart of Stone, 105

Heavenly Body, 187

Holding On, 260

How Evolution Came to Indiana, 158

How My Light Is Spent, 161

How to Live, 244

Hunkydoria Euphoria, 157

If Martha Is a Model Mother-in-Law, She Is Definitely the Latest Model, 113

In Andalucía, 142

In Two Degrees of Cold, 116

Jesus, 233

Jonah, 214

Judas, 227

Kicking Sea Urchins, 54

Kind of Fruitfulness, A, 118

Kissing the Aborigines, 236

Kites on a Windy Day, 13

Knight's Tale, The, 12

Land of Cold Sun, 50

Landing Pattern, 53

Last Lines for a Baritone, 37

Last-Minute Message for a Time Capsule, 202

Lighting Your Birthday Cake, 232

Love in the Rain, 120

Love Poem, 99

Martha, 230

Mary, 221

Memo to the 21st Century, 46

Message, 80

Middle of the Night, 25

Mr. Extinction, Meet Ms. Survival, 159

Murder, 82

Never-Never Land, 250

New Year's Resolution, 63

Night Thoughts, 208

Noah, 178

Nobody Dies in the Spring, 48

Nostalgie de la Boue, 128

October Spring, 59

Old Thing, 42

On a Morning Full of Sun, 93

On the *Beagle*, 164

On the Via Veneto, 5

Our Tree, 197

Path of Renunciation, The, 30

Peace with Honor, 95

Persistence of Memory, The, 94

Pill and the Hundred Yard Dash, The, 60

Poem for St. Valentine's Day, A, 24

Possessed, 243

Priest Forever, A, 251

Promise, A, 11

Rabbit, The, 153

Red Kite, 76

Remembering the Great Depression, 14

Revision, 74

Revolution, 79

Sarah, 189

Savior, 104

Scrapbook, 121

"Sea Otter Survival Assured," 162

Seeing into Bedrooms, 65

Sensual Music, 196

Serpent, 73

Skeletons of Dreams, The, 126

Snow on the Bosporus, 6

State of Nature, 132

Success Story, 18

Summer Love and Surf, 27

Superstition, 242

Sweet Life, 38

Ten Definitions of Lifetime, 51

Tennis Player Waits for What Waits for
     the Tennis Player, The, 75

Them, 237

Things to Do with Railroads, 16

Thinking of Noubli Laroussi, 31

This Moment, 111

Thought for Suse Pollak, A, 36

Three Haiku, Two Tanka, 33

To the Garbage Collectors in
     Bloomington, Indiana, the First
     Pickup of the New Year, 20

To the River, 3

Town and Gown, 43

Trickle-Down Theory of Happiness,
     The, 201

Truth, 70

Vasectomy, 256

Vigil, 9

Voyage Home, The, 166

Waiting for the Fire, 98

Waldorf-Astoria Euphoria, 155

Watching Her Sleep, 211

Westhampton Cemetery, 71

What the U.S. Bureau of Customs Will
     Cry at Public Auction on June 5, 56

Will, 258

Word to Socrates, A, 35

Worm, The, 152

You Said, That's the Fourth Bird This
     Year to Hit Our Picture Window, 39

"Your Papers, Please", 67

ABOUT THE AUTHOR

PHILIP APPLEMAN is the author of six earlier books of poetry, among which are *Let There Be Light* (HarperCollins, 1991) and *Darwin's Ark* (Indiana University Press, 1984); three novels, including *Apes and Angels* (Putnam, 1989) and *Shame the Devil* (Crown, 1981); and several nonfiction books, including the widely read Norton Critical Edition, *Darwin*, as well as the Norton Critical Edition of Malthus' treatise on overpopulation. His work has received many honors, among them a fellowship in poetry from the National Endowment for the Arts, the Society of Midland Authors Poetry Award, the Friends of Literature Poetry Award, both the Morley and the Castagnola Award from the Poetry Society of America, and the American Humanist Association Arts Award. His poems have appeared in numerous periodicals, including the *American Review, Harper's Magazine, Massachusetts Review, The Nation, New Republic, New York Quarterly, New York Times, North American Review, Paris Review, Partisan Review, Poetry, Poetry Northwest, Sewanee Review, Tri-Quarterly,* and *Yale Review.*

Appleman served in the U.S. Army Air Corps during World War II and in the merchant marine after the war. He then earned a bachelor's degree from Northwestern University and a master's degree from the University of Michigan, after which he won a Fulbright Fellowship for graduate study at the University of Lyon, France, and then returned to Northwestern for his Ph.D. He was appointed Professor of English at Indiana University and, while there, was a founding editor of the scholarly journal *Victorian Studies,* chaired the graduate creative writing program, and was awarded a Distinguished Professorship. He was also Visiting Scholar at New York University, Long Island University, and the University of Southern California, twice directed the International Honors Program, an around-the-world year of college study, and has been Visiting Professor at Columbia University and at the State University of New York.

He is married to the playwright and poet Marjorie (M. H.) Appleman, and lives on Long Island and in New York City. His autobiography recently appeared in *Contemporary Authors.*

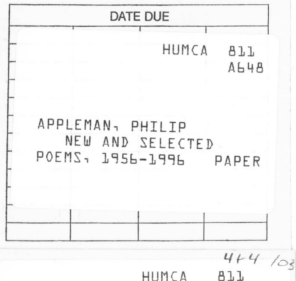